WHY
BUSH
MUST
GO

To the Memory of
Mohandas K. Gandhi
(1869–1948)

whose surpassing vision and use of nonviolence
as a world-transforming power altered permanently
the human spiritual and political pilgrimage.

WHY
BUSH
MUST
GO

A Bishop's
Faith-Based Challenge

Bennett J. Sims

continuum
NEW YORK • LONDON

2004

The Continuum International Publishing Group Inc
15 East 26th Street, New York, NY 10010

The Continuum International Publishing Group Ltd
The Tower Building, 11 York Road, London SE1 7NX

www.continuumbooks.com

All biblical quotations are from the New Revised Standard Version
unless otherwise noted.

Library of Congress Cataloging-in-Publication Data

Sims, Bennett J., 1920–
    Why Bush must go : a bishop's faith-based challenge /
  Bennett J. Sims.
        p.   cm.
    Includes bibliographical references.
    ISBN 0-8264-1637-3 (hardcover : alk. paper)
    1. Christianity and politics—United States. 2. United
  States—Politics and government—2001– I. Title.
  BR526.S576 2004
  261.7′0973–dc22

                        2004006831

The author has named the Institute for Servant Leadership as
recipient of all royalties.

Contents

Preamble

On January 20, 1989, on the west steps of the Capitol George H. W. Bush prayed his own inaugural prayer. It was succinct and true. *"Heavenly Father, we bow our heads and thank you for your love. Accept our thanks for the peace that yields this day and the shared faith that makes its continuance likely. Make us strong to do your work, willing to hear and heed your will, and write on our hearts these words: 'Use power to help people.' For we are given power not to advance our own purposes, nor to make a great show in the world, nor a name. There is but one just use of power, and it is to serve people. Help us to remember, Lord. Amen."*

Preface

The Politics of
Peril and Promise

*We do not say that a man who takes no interest in pol-
itics is a man who minds his own business; we say that
he has no business here at all.*

—Pericles of Athens, fifth century BCE

DURING WORLD WAR II, when I served as a line
officer on destroyers, I was proud of my country
and my government. Only months before the war ended
President Franklin Roosevelt died, and I mourned. In
his wake Harry Truman proved a leader to stir American confidence and pride. This was especially true in the
aftermath of the war when, under Truman, my government confounded all traditions of conquest by installing
the Marshall Plan to capitalize and rebuild the countries
just conquered. This momentous break with the traditional politics of vengeance was my first awakening to
the connection between a high-hearted spirituality and
the realism of political practice.

During the cold war, the ominous threat of Soviet military aggressiveness forced a sharp shift in the politics
of American leadership. We became defensively aggressive, building a counterthreatening arsenal of more

7

powerful nuclear weaponry and installing a policy of
first-strike privilege. We entered upon several unwin-
nable military adventures, notably, in Vietnam, where
we abandoned our folly only after sacrificing literally
countless lives on both sides of the conflict, running
for cover. When, in 1989–1991, the Soviet Communist
tyranny collapsed from within, my country behaved as
if the security threat remained undiminished. We kept
on building and refining our nuclear arsenal, never re-
pudiating our first-strike policy. Now, under a political
leadership of unilateral military adventuring, my country is awash in federal budget deficits to advance an
already overblown military establishment in support of
a world-resisted invasion of Iraq while enduring, so far,
the embarrassing inability to conquer the conquered. I
continue to cherish a patriot pride in my country, but in
my government I have lost all confidence.

What follows in this book is an attempt to write
truthfully and hopefully about the present and future of the human pilgrimage. From my perspective
on history, the truth is that the political leadership
of my country has become a menace to the longevity
of the human and environmental odysseys by several
reckless moves. They are (1) unilateral warmaking in
a time that calls for international peace-seeking collaboration, (2) lavishly heightened investment in the
military, (3) consequent impoverishment of education
and health care for American citizens, (4) scorn of
environmental constraints and global treaties, (5) pref-
erential economic treatment for the wealthy and select
corporations, and (6) the beginning erosion of constitutional guarantees of citizen freedom.

The hope is that, by the timing of God's sovereignty, evolving human consciousness has reached a massive point of turning. By many signs we are both pained and privileged to live on a great hinge of history that is shifting the balance of global leadership from warfare to negotiation as the way to peace. Following millennia of violence as the prime conflict resolution mechanism, human sensitivity is now moving toward a renewal of an even older recourse to nonviolence as the way to compose the inevitable clashes of personal and public wills. Chapters that follow will cite the evidence of an older and infinitely more peaceable norm of human behavior that has come to light in archaeological digs and research into human prehistory. Meanwhile, the radically opposing engines of human striving, violence and nonviolence, constitute the political peril and promise of our moment in time.

God's sovereignty is active in human affairs to direct the course of history, but always at the cost of honoring the freedom and risk of human impulse and deciding. There is often great subtlety about the way God works to bring light from darkness. This subtlety was evident in the way that Richard Nixon's suppression of truth was all but accidentally brought to light with Alexander Butterfield's surprise disclosure about the presidential tapes. This same subtlety may now be on the horizon of contemporary events. There appears to be a rising tide of suspicion that the Bush administration was in possession of intelligence that warned of the 9/11 terrorist attacks on New York and Washington. It may be that this warning information was not only disregarded, but that investigations into the matter were actually obstructed to serve American political designs. Eventually the truth will out, and for the sake of national honor one may hope that we are not on the threshold of another devastating disclosure.

Whether or not there was calculated neglect of danger by our government, the question itself exposes the larger issue, which is that the key to understanding this capital moment in the long human pilgrimage lies in the meaning and use of power. The sciences of archaeology and paleontology assign roughly the last 100,000 years to the emergence of advanced human consciousness. In all but the most recent tiny segment of that great span we seem to have intuited power as the impulse to live collaboratively and to settle conflict by nonviolent negotiation.[1] Only since the emergence of conquest clans and empires, somewhere between 6000 and 4000 BCE (or about 6,000 to 8,000 years ago), does it appear that our understanding and exercise of power turned from cooperation to competition, from partnership to domination, from nonviolence to calculated aggression and warfare. Since that shift from partnership to dominance in the understanding and use of power, it is clear that history has been singularly unkind to "male-dominant" empire building. Domination models are all dead and displaced — from Egypt and Babylon to Nazi Germany and Communist Russia. The old and recent empires are all gone, and history will surely be no kinder to American imperial designs. But hope blossoms in the growing worldwide revulsion from superpower swagger and an aroused conviction that violence only compounds the very violence it seeks to subdue. These emergent impulses at home and abroad signal the moving hand of divine Providence.

In my darkest foreboding about the future of the world I am daily heartened by the conviction that, at deep levels of the human psyche, we are moving toward a recovery of our earliest intuition about power. Many say that we have been so moving, and very slowly, since a time in history that some scholars have called the "axial age" of human consciousness. They apply the term *axial* to the years 800 to 600 BCE. This critical cluster of years marks the conscious reemergence of the dynamic of nonviolence in the teachings of the Buddha and by the piercing thunder of the Hebrew prophets. Rabbi Abraham Heschel wrote, "When the prophets appeared they proclaimed that might is not supreme, that the sword is an abomination, that violence is obscene. The sword, they said, shall be destroyed."[2]

For Christians, the peak flowering of nonviolent wisdom and sacrifice emerged in the brief and momentous ministry of an earlier and ever-present rabbi, Jesus of Nazareth. Jesus situated his call to nonviolence on the long continuum of history, making it clear that his summons represented a decisive break with conventional human behavior. "You have heard that it was said, 'You shall love your neighbor and hate your enemy.' But I say to you, Love your enemies and pray for those who persecute you.…"[3] While this is now a distinctly Christian admonition, it is important to note that all the great religions of the world posit a variant of the Golden Rule as a distillation of their ethics.

By contrast with the years of my military service (1943–1946), my country now pursues policies that exacerbate the peril to God's world by an imperialist violence that the great religions have long repudiated. This must become plain and urgent to the American electorate, or the planet and all forms of its life face a darkening horizon. This book is written as a call to understand that power and politics are two sides of the same coin, that political action always reflects a people's belief about power, and that political conviction and decision making are sacramental embodiments of a nation's spiritual makeup. Perhaps never before in American history have partisan political differences clashed so sharply as now over the critical decisions about the use of our nation's power. Given the ever-growing belief in America and the world community in the nonviolent use of power, this book hopes to encourage a use of the voting booth to replace the self-destructive course that controversially elected political leadership has chosen for our country.

Such a book is a brash and unconventional note for an old cleric to sound. It will be objected that I am mixing religion and politics. But of course. This mixture has always been the implicit ground of all political action, and it is in high public fashion now. We need only ask the present incumbent of the Oval Office about his blend of politics and religion. He has said that God has called him to be president of the United States. And he is so confident of divine appointment as to hold in scorn the bulk of American and world religious leadership, including Pope John Paul II and the Dalai Lama, when he refused, without apology, to listen to their ardent opposition to the military invasion of Iraq.

This book confronts two huge problems. The first is personal; the second is conceptual. The personal difficulty is that, in arguing for the replacement of President Bush and his administration, I risk the very spiritual malady of contempt for the opposition that afflicts the motives and moves of present political leadership. The liturgical usage of my church offers a measure of protection against capitulation to countercontempt in our tradition of prayer for "The President of the United States and all in Civil Authority," in the Book of Common Prayer. Phillips Brooks (1835–1893), the rector of Trinity Church, Boston, and later bishop of Massachusetts, wrote, "We cannot be at enmity with any one whose advocate we are before the throne of Grace." It is my hope that these pages can be clean of acrimony. At a deeper and more personal level, I have added an appendix to this book that commends a series of personal resolutions, plus a twelve-step spiritual discipline and a litany designed to gird the human heart for Servanthood. These are offered as resources for Servant Leadership in such goodwill as adds energy to the momentum of nonviolence that now mounts for justice and peace.

The conceptual problem is that there are two antithetical power motifs in the religions of the world: the conventional dominator drive and the visionary collaborative ideal. The first version carries the name fundamentalism. It is locked into an old and ebbing form of human consciousness that urges the use of violence — to avenge violence — as in the "eye for an eye" moral dictum. By contrast, at the heart of all the world's religions there is voice that knows counterviolence to be counterproductive. In the first version there is a strain of eager attachment to things as they are, along with the impulse to obey unquestioningly the constituted authorities, including punitive and jealous deities of wrath. But this is not the evolving heart of the great religions. The social historian Riane Eisler writes,

> [Vengeance] is not the spirituality of the great religious visionaries of history. Isaiah and Jesus, Gautama and Hildegard of Bingen did not ask us to tolerate injustice and cruelty. They tried to change things. Jesus stopped the stoning of a woman and Hildegard stood up to a pope. At the core of the major faiths—Hindu, Buddhist, Muslim, Christian and Confucian—are the partnership values of sensitivity, empathy, caring and nonviolence.[4]

Fundamentalist religion is cast in the ancient maledominant tradition and is preoccupied with an imminent and violent end of the world. Here it follows naturally that getting to heaven is a paramount concern, while world resources, as long as they last, can be exploited for the special gain of the faithful. By contrast, a nonliteralist and biblically profound Christianity understands the central petition of the Lord's Prayer as a manifesto: "Thy Kingdom come, thy will be done *on earth* as it is in Heaven." This places a firm priority on the life of the world, not on heaven—which the Lord's Prayer presumes can take heavenly care of itself. Such a clear priority on the world instantly translates into a religiously charged personal, economic, and political mission to extend the evolving life of the planet in justice and peace as God-intended gifts for all God-created forms of life.

Of course, both forms of religion are subject to gross error. I understand evil as the calculated sundering of God's cosmic union that holds the web of life in intricate interdependence; it remains a perverse power to bedevil the human spirit and all religions. This is evidenced in Christian history by the brutal violence of medieval Europe with the Crusades and in colonial America with the burning of witches and in contemporary fundamentalist forms of Islam. But the antidote to violence-prone religions and their politics of violence is the application of Mohandas Gandhi's wisdom. He understood that the politics of freedom rise from visionary and compassionate religion, as in the development of the American constitution and its provision for democratic balance and the sharing of power. Gandhi also understood that the power of nonviolent spirituality and steadfastness can bring about the justice and peace for which all the major religions teach their adherents to pray. The nonviolent departure of Britain from India in 1947 proved the truth of Gandhi's beliefs.

H. L. Mencken, a caustic writer and a debunker of hypocrisy and deceit, once said that one of his books was a one-way ticket to hell. This book may earn me such a one-way ticket in the assessment of many, but silence can be seditious. Silence in the face of what I perceive to be dire peril ought to entitle me to first-class passage to outer darkness. This was the hope of some Episcopalians in Georgia, who counted me correctly as an enemy of some capital forms of the status quo—forms like racial segregation, our medieval Prayer Book of 1928, and priesthood as the exclusive domain of privileged males. But looking back at my dozen years as a diocesan Episcopal bishop in the 1970s and 1980s, they are years of growing up fast in a privileged and learning journey.

The personal odyssey covered in this book begins with the Episcopal Diocese of Atlanta in 1972. It was then that my understanding of the rising tide of American militarism began as a cloud on the horizon during the early arms race, becoming a darkening sky in the Reagan years and mounting as a tempest since the inauguration of George W. Bush. As I write in protest of the steady march of violence as political policy in my country, my severest problem is how to avoid nursing a counterviolence in myself. In arguing for nonviolence, I can be convincing only as I am able, in the wisdom of Jesus, to be aware of the plank in my own eye[5] while seeking removal of the blinding splinters in the eyes of a fundamentalist-driven administration. This is the importance of the spiritual resources in the appendix of this book.

Several great friends have encouraged me in fashioning the chapters that follow. They include my brother, Edward R. Sims, a gifted and distinguished retired priest of the Episcopal Church; Isabel Carter Heyward, a professor of theology at the Episcopal Divinity School in Cambridge, Massachusetts; Marcus J. Borg, a professor of religion and culture at Oregon State University; my brilliant successor as president of the Institute for Servant Leadership, Deacon Bill Jamieson; and my continuing colleague from our "bishoping" days, the Right

Reverend William H. Folwell, retired bishop of Central Florida and golf partner in these later years. Others include John K. Moore and his wife, Patricia, who have been lavishly supportive of the Institute for Servant Leadership and of me. Frank Oveis, senior editor at Continuum, has smoothed and sharpened this book. I owe him a great debt. Finally, as with so many who write books, it is my wife who has given the most encouragement and helpful critique. Mary Page and I, married now for fifteen years, share two uncontrived gifts. The first is that we have the same birthday, August 9, although I arrived twenty-two years earlier. The other gift rises from a gracious source far deeper than coincidence. Our mystic gift is that both of us have reached maturity in second marriages and have never known such an abundance of easy friendship, love, and joy.

B. J. S.

Chapter One

Saints and Sinners

You will realize that doctrines are the inventions of the human mind, as it tries to penetrate the mysteries of God.

—Pelagius, Celtic Christian theologian, fifth century CE

THE EPISCOPAL DIOCESE OF ATLANTA is the child of a 1907 decision to slice the Diocese of Georgia in half. The parent jurisdiction, founded in 1841 and which compassed the entire state, became too large for a single bishop to visit all his parishes in a single year. The line that separated the new diocese from the old is an undulating horizontal S curve that loops north and east from the Alabama border below Columbus to a point on the South Carolina border above Augusta. This division of geography was decided on the basis of its making the two dioceses about equal in population. Time since then has ballooned the northern of the two jurisdictions all out of proportion to its original size. The Diocese of Atlanta has become a territory of one supreme urban density and several lesser urban vitalities with suburban sprawl and commercial vigor — and all without losing the rural flavor of the Old South slouch and drawl.

Back in 1907 a special organizing committee pre-
sented the Convention of the parent diocese with two
possible names for the new jurisdiction. The delegates
could choose between the Diocese of North Georgia and
the Diocese of Atlanta, after its principal city. It is widely
believed now that no fit Southerner could then choose
a name that included the word *north* so soon after the
ignominy of the South at the hands of Mr. Lincoln's
armies.

The bishop of Georgia was then Cleland Kinloch Nelson, the first of two "Yankees" summoned South to lead
a diocese in Georgia. I was the second. Bishop Nelson, from Bethlehem, Pennsylvania, was consecrated
in 1892 and fifteen years later opted to become the
first bishop of the new diocese. He served as bishop of
Atlanta until his death ten years later, in 1917. Imme-
diately upon his arrival in 1892, as the new Yankee in
Georgia, C. K. Nelson was confronted with a controversial change in the liturgical patterns of the whole
church. A revised prayer book was mandated by the
1892 General Convention to supersede the original
prayer books of 1785 and 1789 in the newly formed
Protestant Episcopal Church in the United States of
America. The 1892 revision was still a medievalist version of the piety and prayers of the old book, but
it did replace the cherished manual of devotion used
by all Episcopalians for 103 years — and especially by
Robert E. Lee all his life. For a "Yankee" to declare
the great general's prayer book out of order must have
been bitter medicine, especially since the newly arrived Bishop Nelson circulated a rather bluntly worded

pastoral directive that forbade the further use of the old book as soon as copies of the new one were in hand.

All five of my predecessors as bishop of Atlanta faced the tribulation of change in both church and society, especially my immediate predecessor, Randolph R. Claiborne Jr. It was he who bore the opening brunt of the most convulsive social controversy of the twentieth century, the era of Atlanta's most esteemed son, the Reverend Dr. Martin Luther King Jr. Bishop Claiborne bequeathed to me a heritage of honor for having faced bravely the firestorm of racial integration. He served for nineteen difficult years and died at age eighty in 1986. I wish that he had left us a written record of his moral wrestling with such tensions as Dr. King's attempt to enroll his children in the all-white Lovett School in upscale suburban Atlanta. Lovett was founded with organic connections to the Diocese of Atlanta, but when the school's board of trustees refused to honor the application for admission by the King children, Bishop Claiborne cut all the school's ties to the diocese. Instantly he was bitterly condemned for offending the sensibilities of cultural privilege. He wore thereafter the prickly badge of honor that was mine to wear for my own several offenses to Southern comfort as his successor.

FOR ME, THE MOST IMPORTANT GAIN in the subsequent heavy changes was the subtle emergence of a fresh theology — a theology that takes seriously God's gift of all-inclusive human dignity and moral freedom. At the deepest and most enduring level of human understanding that theological shift represents a seismic change in our understanding of power. For all the centuries of war-dominated recorded history humankind has conceived of power as "dominance from above." That continues to be the singular dictionary definition of the word *power.* In spite of the stubborn "power as control" mindset perpetuated in the aggressive militarism of prevailing American political policy, the human pilgrimage has begun to advance on the leading edge of a new conception of power as "relationships of equality." Given now the "dominating" human technical skill not only to despoil the earth but also to incinerate our only resource base, *the future will never again come automatically.* A more mature humanity must now *create* the future, or there will be none for much of the planet's abundance of life. And nothing now seems more unlikely of accomplishment, given the patriotic jingoism of present superpower behavior.

American world leadership is now fiercely committed to budget-busting military "dominance from above." In my view, this represents a reversion to an era of adolescence in the evolving human odyssey,[1] and a majority of the American electorate may be supportive of imperial conquest as the answer to the terrorist threat — a threat, moreover, that is not diminished but only compounded by American commitment to the "power of dominance." Given these realities, how can the human future be anything but foreclosed in an apocalyptic nuclear calamity? Still I am hopeful. God is not mocked. My better sense is that a global calamity is only a "short-run" forecast of despair. Beneath the surface of the presently popular "cowboy strut" of American flag waving there moves a rising tide of conflict resolution by the wisdom of nonviolence, a world-preserving use of power in "relationships of equality." Quiet evidence abounds that humanity is on an incipient spiritual move upward, up from the lower conception of power as unilateral privilege to the more mature conception of power as relational equality.

ALL THE CONVULSIONS of societal and ecclesiastical change through which the diocese went in my twelve years as bishop were in honor of the higher value of relational power. There are at least four: (1) civil rights for a hitherto oppressed minority, (2) ordination rights for a theretofore second-class feminine half of the human species, (3) new prayer rites for growing numbers of the Episcopal Church's faithful who were disenchanted with many medieval forms of a rigid worship book, and (4) the equality movement to endow with dignity and freedom the age-long repressed minority whose birth-bestowed gender orientation compels a same-sex attraction. The action of the Episcopal Church's General Convention in mid-2003 to ratify an openly gay priest, the Reverend V. Gene Robinson, to be bishop of New Hampshire leads the way for other church bodies to resolve their equivalent controversies. In the last half-century most Christian bodies have grown younger in social courage than in all the post-Reformation centuries and, perhaps, since the fateful fourth century. That was when the boldness of the early Christian community suffered an enervating top-down takeover by the Emperor Constantine and an almost instant reduction of church freedom to resist the forces of cultural captivity to hierarchical organization and privilege —

and neglect of justice for the poor and marginalized. Were it not for the concurrent emergence of the monastic movement in the fourth century as a counterbalance to Christian worldly indulgence, the apostolic movement of Christ would have derailed into oblivion as a force for justice and peace in society. Thus, as I have grown old, my church has grown young, because the Episcopal Church in the half century of my own ministry has regrown the moral muscle to stand and suffer for social justice and endure schisms in consequence.

THERE HAVE BEEN EVEN WIDER and more collective evidences of emerging social courage and justice making. They burst into view in 1947 with the collaborative departure of the British Raj from India after 250 years of "dominance from above." Many previous years of rising nonviolent pressure under the leadership of Gandhi finally forced the British colonial administrative and military presence to leave India in total nonviolent compliance. In 1989–1991, under the inspiration of Soviet leader Mikhail Gorbachev, the nations of Eastern Europe regained their freedom in a nonviolent revolution after seventy years of ruthless "dominance from above" by the Soviet Union. In April 1994 in South Africa, a long-dominant white minority surrendered political sovereignty to a black majority in a nonviolent exchange of power by popular democratic vote. All these are contemporary nonviolent triumphs of the mature power of relational equality. There are more to come as the world community achieves greater interdependence and less tolerance of minority concentrations of wealth—but only if the momentum of a higher human consciousness can increase faster than the stubborn fear of change.

WHEN IN THE COURSE OF HISTORY the collective ascent into a more mature humanity first appeared is unclear, but in Judeo-Christian tradition the spirit is evident as far back as two familiar poetic Old Testament passages that forecast a transformation of the weapons of conquest into instruments of cultivation and nurture. These are the "swords into plowshares" images of Isaiah 2:4 and Micah 4:3. This change in human valuing has not yet come to pass except in isolated religious and political cases. I have in mind the nonviolent Society of Friends (Quakers) — part of the seventeenth-century persecuted religious outbreak in England — and the total absence of a military establishment since 1948 in the tiny Central American nation of Costa Rica. But everywhere, for leading-edge Christians, this life-giving perception of power came to brilliant flower in the teachings and self-giving servant life of Jesus of Nazareth. And it triumphed in an Easter Cross planted since on the skyline of the world.

True power henceforward, as pockets of human understanding slowly grasp it, means the calling forth of powers in the human spirit created in the image of God. The political formation of this fresh truth about power is democracy, but because it stands as a fairly recent historical corrective to "power as dominance," it continues to be imperiled by resurgences of male-dominant passion — a reaction of fear over the erosion of imperial male privileges. As was introduced in the foreword, we know this reaction in religious and political terms by the name fundamentalism, which, in all its "power as dominance" forms, has become the great backward-facing force in our time. It uses terrorism as a worldwide instrument of intimidation and subjugation. In the United States the fundamentalist surge seeks to reverse the course of history, seizing the levers of unilateral power in a heavily militarized government, which, by all its signs, seeks the reduction of democratic protections and their replacement by a world-dominating imperialism.

Fundamentalism would have a hard time with the title of this chapter. It would omit the word *saint* and include only the word *sinner* as describing a naturally depraved humanity. In Christian fundamentalist theology there is no such dual description of humankind. All are born sinners. Apart from a decision by human initiative to reach for rebirth as a "born again" person, sainthood has no broad common reality. In sharp contrast, George Fox, the Quaker reformer, called all these doctrinal deductions "notions" and leaned toward a sunnier view of the human makeup. He is best known for his conviction that, as he put it, "there is that of God in everyone." Long before Fox the Christian tradition was enriched by the Celtic stream of influence as defined very early on by the Welsh monk Pelagius, whose time in history spanned the late fourth and early fifth centuries. Celtic theology is happy with the natural paradox of "saint and sinner." It uses this duality to describe all of humanity from start to finish, especially from the start. Created in God's own image, according to Genesis 1:27, there is a deposit of unadulterated goodness at the core of each human being. Pelagius deduced from both Scripture and his own beholding of humanity that, despite the evil impulses that overtake all human willing, an original goodness endures at the heart of each human being. My sense of the truth of original goodness is confirmed by two human impulses that act as rebuttals to the Augustinian-Calvinist doctrine of invincible depravity.

The first rebutting impulse is what Carl Jung called "projection" — the universal propensity to shift the blame. The blaming impulse is the deeply embedded mechanism that denies any deviation from a created and original goodness. Blaming is the profound ratification of the language of the old confession in our medieval prayer books where penitents say of their sins that "the burden of them is intolerable." This language precisely defines the burden of guilt as an offense to the instinctive gift of what some theologies call "original blessing." The second rebuttal to the doctrine of original sin follows upon the first as the impulse to confess. Confession is the painful and ennobling embrace of the reality of brokenness—the brokenness in the fabric of relationships to self, to God, and to significant others. This, more than blaming, is a seal upon the reality of a longing to recover an intended and abandoned goodness. Pelagius held that what we have abandoned is the beauty we behold in every new life fresh to the world. He wrote, "Looking into the face of a newborn child is not to see a soul already corrupted but rather a soul alight with the beauty of God."[2] By such understandings, admitting their controversial character, we are all complex blends of saint and sinner.

Original sin, as the dark definition of humanity, has haunted the Christian pilgrimage ever since it triumphed by the searching power of intellect and self-examination by the bishop of Hippo, St. Augustine (354–430). It continues to commend itself as a valid deduction about our human makeup by virtue of the sharply accusatory character of the human spirit in self-examination — and by the overwhelming evidence of "missing the mark" at every level of advancing human behavior, from the playpen to old age.

Augustine's finely honed sense of shame with regard to his own sexual adventuring as a young man prior to his conversion to Christ and his penetrating insight into pervasive wrongdoing in the world led him to deduce (i.e., invent) the view that, like himself in preconversion lustful indulgence, humanity must be naturally depraved. Furthermore, deducing from his early sexual license, every child is born depraved by the operation of sexual transmission from one generation to the next, from Adam's lust to the present. Augustine, true to his time, regarded the Adam and Eve record as historic reporting, not as a trenchantly true and descriptive myth of enlightened contemporary biblical understanding and exegesis. As a towering thinker, Augustine was deeply shaped by the scriptural writings of St. Paul, especially by Paul's Letter to the Romans. This surpassing document, written in about 56 CE, has made its writer Christianity's foremost theologian and ethicist — to whom and through whom God speaks. Thus, Augustine's doctrine of original sin has held the preeminent place in assessing the basic human makeup in all the centuries since, and especially now in the popular tide of fundamentalism. However, through the centuries there has persisted an underground and sunnier view of humanity as a parallel assessment of basic human character. It relies on an earlier biblical warrant in Genesis than the centuries-later epistles of Paul, and in our time that old underground has begun to break the surface of Christian thinking with the emergence of Pelagian scholarship. The sunnier view of "original righteousness" now challenges the exclusivity of Augustine's hold on orthodoxy.

One of the most distinctive ways to see this emerging challenge by a more cheerful view is to compare the historic versions of the General Confession in the succession of Anglican prayer books with its most recent American revision in 1979. From Archbishop Cranmer's translation from the Latin in 1549 through all later revisions, the General Confession has described humanity in terms of an invincible depravity: *"There is no health in us....Have mercy upon us, miserable offenders....We acknowledge and bewail our manifold sins and wickedness. ...Provoking most justly thy wrath and indignation against us...."*[3] But in our time, and in sharp contrast, the General Confession of Rite II in the American Book of Common Prayer of 1979 never uses words that accent or even suggest "depravity." Instead, it understands sin as the pervasive misuse of human freedom in the tragic failure to love and to reconnect: *"Most merciful God...we have not loved you with our whole heart; we have not loved our neighbors as ourselves. We are truly sorry and humbly repent....Have mercy on us and forgive us; that we may delight in your will and walk in your ways."*[4] Here the capital accent in our Confession has turned from dread of God's wrath to delight in God's will.

WHILE IT WAS OFTEN a severe discomfort to preside over the Diocese of Atlanta during an era of disruptive change, it was a high privilege to have had a small hand in the transformation of a regional section of church and society. In the course of twelve volatile years as bishop, I met many able and courageous apostles of change. With my lights and shadows they were one with me as both saints and sinners. They were clergy and laity, many in my diocese, and many more in other settings and allegiances. The most aggressive apostle of change with whom I was literally forced to deal was a white professor of English in an all-black college in the conservative southern town of Fort Valley, Georgia. He is Professor Louie Crew, founder of the national gay-lesbian support and advocacy group Integrity.

Louie Crew is a man of incisive brilliance. I knew nothing of his presence in the diocese until he appeared on my calendar for an afternoon office appointment in 1974. Speaking plainly and without cordiality, he introduced himself as a gay man whose gay partner was a black hairdresser. He had just founded Integrity as a mission to homosexuals. It was to be a community of encouragement, membership, and national advocacy. He intended it to include all gay and lesbian Episcopalians, hoping for the establishment of Integrity groups in churches and dioceses across the whole Episcopal Church in America. Not bothering with opening courtesies, he confronted me by saying, "Bishop, I am a member of St. Luke's Church in Fort Valley, and I am here to claim the legitimacy of my gay identity and to press for your support of the Integrity movement. Now, what are you going to do about it?" I was stunned. I had not given the issue of homosexuality a second thought since a dimly remembered surreptitious approach by a man in the shadows of a parking lot during my high school days in Kansas City, an approach from which I instinctively withdrew as inappropriate and bewildering. Now, here in the formality of my office and years later, I was confronted with the same reality, but this time with great intelligence and forthrightness. What was I going to do about it, indeed!

That first meeting multiplied into a dozen or more encounters between us, most of them in my office. These encounters grew steadily more confrontational, one of them including his attorney, as Louie pressed for my personal and official acceptance of his sexual orientation and my support of Integrity. Louie's pressure, and my mounting discomfort with his occasional hostility and accusation, forced me into research and writing. I gave the mornings of our family summer vacation of 1977 to fashioning as clear and compassionate a response as I could write. In my 1982 book *Purple Ink,* this came to nineteen pages as a pastoral letter to the churches and communicants of the diocese. In it I drew upon all the thoughtful literature I could find on the pros and cons of homosexuality, using biblical, theological, psychological, ethical, and medical-psychiatric resources. In substance what I wrote was an acceptance of homosexual persons as fully entitled to honorable membership in the church and the resources of its pastoral ministry. However, my research led me to conclude the condition to be, for most homosexuals, amenable to correction by spiritual and therapeutic intervention. The pastoral letter ended with a terse statement that for a homosexual it was entirely acceptable "to be" but equally unacceptable "to do." In other words, my reading and obvious bias led to an acceptance of gay identity but a rejection of gay behavior as disallowed by Christian moral standards.

I intended that pastoral letter for the Diocese of Atlanta only. However, the issue had so much currency in and out of the church that the letter was widely distributed, and I became an instant spokesperson for conservative bias, near and far. The nondenominational periodical *Christianity Today* reprinted it in full. The Lutheran Church in Sweden made it their official position on the issue, printing it in Swedish in their church organ. Not only did the churches of America and overseas applaud the letter, but our own very conservative presiding bishop of the Episcopal Church, John Maury Allin, appointed me chair and principal writer of the pastoral letter committee of our House of Bishops. Over the ensuing five years, with the help of a select committee, I wrote the annual bishops' pastoral letters to all the congregations of the Episcopal Church, and Jack Allin and I became friends. Before that time he and I had kept each other at cool distances.

With all this acceptance from my own church and from most of the ecumenical community, I wondered when the other shoe would drop. When was I going to be sandbagged by gay-lesbian forces, and by Dr. Louie Crew in particular? Only one contrary and contemptuous letter came to me. It was *not* from Louie. By contrast, the Integrity group in the diocese quietly invited me to visit one of their meetings at All Saints

Church in downtown Atlanta and to join them in worship. I did so with some trepidation at first, but later with gratitude and frequency. There I discovered that a few of my ablest clergy were among them, men and women, plus a surprising number of well-placed laity of the city. At every such meeting I was met with warmth and affection. This experience was completely unexpected and mind-opening. The years went by, and my contacts with the gay-lesbian community extended and increased. In time I started over in research and came to a firm conclusion almost the reverse of my earlier view. Homosexuality was an ontological characteristic, as birth-bestowed as skin color and gender identity in the overwhelming majority of gay men and women. Homosexual intimacy was almost never a matter of perverse behavioral choice. It was in response to the engine of sexual desire implanted in all human beings by design. It carried the name "natural," as natural as my maleness and creeping baldness. It was now 1984, and I had retired as bishop at the end of the previous year to become a visiting professor of theology at Emory University and founder of the Institute for Servant Leadership.

Meanwhile, the sexuality issue had heightened to the point of threat to the unity of the Episcopal Church. It was the most bitterly contested concern on the agenda of the forthcoming General Convention, to which eight deputies from the Diocese of Atlanta would be dispatched and voting. Word came to me that some of our deputies held a strong conservative view, and that those on the conservative side of the debate might use their former bishop's 1977 pastoral letter as supporting their position against the moral legitimacy of gays and lesbians. So I wrote another careful pastoral statement that reflected my changed position, intending it for exclusive distribution among the Atlanta deputation to the General Convention. But as before, the statement went far and wide.

It came to Louie's attention, and he phoned me with an outpouring of thanks. By then he had become professor of English at Rutgers University in New Brunswick, New Jersey. Some years later Louie invited me to concelebrate and to speak briefly at Integrity's twentieth anniversary Eucharist, held at the General Convention of 1994 in Indianapolis. That service remains the most spirited and memorable experience of worship in all the years of my ministry. The cathedral was crowded to the extent of its capacity and more. Worshippers stood for nearly two hours beneath the overflowing balcony, many more stood for the long service against the cathedral walls, and still more gathered outside on the street. Louie, in his doctoral gown, preached the sermon. He began with a salute to all of us who had defied the convention's rejection of homosexuality by coming for worship in an alien setting that night. He opened with a great smile, saying, "Welcome to Samaria!"

It needs to be emphasized that my change of heart and mind was not the work of reading and distant research. I believe that it had its beginning years before in a totally unanticipated moment of seeing Louie in a different and deeper light. We were in my office for the umpteenth time one afternoon, and he was talking. Suddenly, as a kind of interior flash of recognition, I felt a current of affection for him. He and I were kindred, not in sexual orientation, but in our shared and struggling humanity. That must have been the opening moment of seeing the courage and authenticity of a man of sharply different sexual drive. It was a drive that neither of us had created but only claimed as an expression of God's design of sexuality across all the divides in the anciently evolving family of life. That experience of seeing authentic humanity and goodness in a person of very different sexual impulses was repeated and multiplied in later years as I met with the Integrity group at All Saints Church. In other words, I was not persuaded to alter my position simply by thinking; *I was changed by interactive human experience.* By the mounting warmth of interpersonal trust, I was moved by the power of affection to abandon the notion of domination from above in favor of the far higher motivational ground of relationships in equality.

In 1997 I published my third book, *Servanthood: Leadership for the Third Millennium,* and in it is a chapter that elaborates my experience of inner change with all the supporting conceptual evidence that I could bring to bear. The chapter, titled "Servanthood and Sexual Ethics," however, does not include my most recent conceptual discovery that goes to the meaning of a key word in Paul's letter to the Romans. The word in English is *natural,* and it occurs in two connecting verses, Romans 1:26–27, that those who reject homosexual legitimacy rely on heavily. Importantly, St. Paul never uses the term *homosexuality* in those verses, however that word might have been translated in his uniform use of Greek. In explicitly condemning homosexual behavior, he argues that it is not *physikos,* which in English is translated as "natural," or more elaborately, as "produced by nature," "inborn," or "agreeable to nature."[5] For Paul, *physikos* surely meant "heterosexual" and nothing else. For him, it was not "natural" that women should engage sexually with women or men with men. But today, in the latest medical research and understanding of homosexuality, this orientation is believed to be established very early in the human fetus by a process known as the "sexing of the brain." This process is connected to the level of testosterone, the male hormone, in the pregnant female and sexual identity once established is, in the opinion of credible medical research, not changeable.

In his autobiography Bishop John Shelby Spong quotes Dr. Robert Lahita, a close friend and researcher at Cornell Medical Center in New York. Dr. Lahita's research leads him to contend that, as Jack puts it, "all human beings have one sex organ, the brain. All else is equipment."[6] Insofar as this is physiologically certain, then, the Greek term *physikos* can be recomprehended, making St. Paul's polemical use of it far too limiting and understandably wrong in his contention that homosexuality is not natural. As a bestowed sexual identity, in utero homosexuality becomes ontological, on the order of a natural endowment. Once this interpretation of *physikos* is accepted, it becomes possible, even necessary in sound biblical scholarship, to argue that in an uncertain proportion of humanity (and perhaps in lower animals also) homosexuality is a naturally occurring reality, and that whatever one's given sexuality, the critical matter is how that natural drive is expressed.

The Christian sexual ethic holds that for either hetero- or homosexual identity, promiscuity, perversity, and all exploitative and dominating relationships are morally out of order. They are prohibited because such behavioral choices degrade our created humanity. Our souls are fashioned in the image of God, both in freedom and in righteousness. The emblem of God's righteousness in human makeup is the mystery of "conscience" that whispers what is right and wrong in the exercise of human freedom. The freedom of moral choice may be nowhere more severely challenged than in dealing with the clamoring engine of sexual appetite. Built in God's image for obedience to the best, the whispers of conscience will, sooner or later, bring regret and remorse over the misuses of sex in recreational lust, in betrayal of vows, or in exploitative male-dominance, of which rape is the towering malfeasance. By contrast, the whispers of conscience in obedience to the best bring the deep resonances of happiness and fulfillment in sexual relationships of intimate mutuality and singular monogamous fidelity. *Relational equality is the wholeness for which humanity is made.*

Chapter Two

Competition Superseded

People often say that they enjoy competing but then change their minds when they learn firsthand what it's like to work or play in a setting that does not require winners and losers.

—Robert Helmreich, professor, University of Texas, 1986

O NE OF MY MOST VALUED RECOLLECTIONS involves a thirty-seven-page booklet that arrived with the office mail in 1974, two years after I took up work as a bishop. The little publication was titled *The Servant as Leader,* by Robert K. Greenleaf. How it happened to come to me I have never known, and why I took the time, then and there, to read it is an enduring mystery. My habit with mailed pamphlets is either to toss them quickly aside or to dump them in the wastebasket. It must have been the arresting paradox of the title that moved me. Conceptually, practically, and even spatially, the words *servant* and *leader,* when juxtaposed, are nonsense. Intellectually, the two words are mutually exclusive, sharply contradictory. In practice, leading means taking charge, not bending in servitude. In spatial imagery, a leader is positioned above and ahead, while a servant stands below and behind. Why, then, did that contradictory title draw me into reading what lay beyond it? For three reasons, as I look back on the timing and reconstruct my interior sense of readiness.

First, because I knew I needed help in handling a huge new responsibility. I was the elected leader of a voluntary regional institution spread over 27,000 square miles, comprised of roughly 25,000 Episcopalians in seventy-six loosely linked nonprofit units overseen by more than one hundred priests and their lay leaders. In quiet moments of reflection the magnitude of the task gave me the willies. Second, I believed that my first obligation as bishop was to my clergy. They were key to the vitality of those seventy-six congregations, and all the clergy suffered the same occasional willies as my own as they faced the magnitude of their tasks. Unless I could muster a sturdy "serving" care for each of them, I would only lock myself and them into mutual isolation and varying degrees of vocational fright. Third, there was that bewitching text in Matthew and Mark that confounds all human ambition. Overhearing a dispute about who stood the tallest in the hierarchy of his disciples, Jesus gently rebuked them with a bewildering formula for preeminence: "Whoever wishes to be great among you must be your servant, and whoever wishes to be first among you must be the slave of all."[1] Servant Leadership is clearly the first principle of being in charge of anything as a Christian. How could I *not* read the pamphlet?

It turned out to be hard reading, but its author carried all the important credentials as a wise and experienced manager of people. In his business life, Bob Greenleaf, was highly placed as the executive in charge of all management development for what was then the largest corporation in the world, American Telephone and Telegraph, before its dismantling into several regional and autonomous corporations. He had been reared a Quaker in Indiana, became an engineer after studying at Carleton College in Minnesota and had risen to a place of high eminence in the management ranks of AT&T. He never worked anywhere else. He was now retired and busy writing trenchant essays on the broad issues of management and leadership. That morning in 1974, I read his pamphlet with rising excitement and delight. He was saying what I knew viscerally to be true about effective leadership, but it was not the most lucid writing. It was sometimes difficult to follow the sequence of his thought, but what he put into words galvanized my resolve to shape my "bishoping" to the ancient Christian formula for the work of leading. More than that, it aroused a sense of wistful longing to be a teacher again. I had come to the diocese from a faculty post at the Virginia Theological Seminary, which I relished.

Prompted by this indelible sense of a vocation to teach, I started a series of learning retreats for regional clusters of the clergy, assuming again the role of seminar teacher in a pattern of mutual exchange. A group facilitator joined me as a staff person in each of these groups, and things went well. Hierarchical barriers between bishop and priests began to melt. By sharing our thoughts and our personal innerness, we warmed to each other. Even better, competitive barriers diminished between clergy in big parishes and little parishes, in city and county, of high church and low church persuasion — all these distinctions, while remaining real, receded in favor of relationships of trust and even affection. My only regret with respect to this program of interactive learning was that it began to give way before the demands of the office for administration and, particularly, for fund-raising. The diocese was growing apace with the rapid expansion of metro Atlanta. We needed a very large helping of new money in cash and greatly increased investment funds for land and buildings and, especially, for the educational and pastoral development of the clergy, both before and following ordination.

Fund-raising is an institutional demand that the top leader of a nonprofit cannot shirk except in peril of losing institutional momentum. It can and must, to some extent, be delegated, but without vigorous cheerleading and a push from the principal leader, fundraising will falter. Fortunately, I enjoyed pushing for funds. Money raised is a concrete measure of achievement, superficial in some sense, but it is an outward and visible sign of energy successfully applied. More than that, it goes to the heart of what I believe is the deepest satisfaction that attaches to money, namely the glow of giving it away.

There is a personal story here worth telling. About halfway through the years of my ministry, I faced the need to launch a fund-raiser for some good reason, and I quailed before it. I hated asking people for money. I must have nursed that resistance for days, maybe weeks, until suddenly something clicked into consciousness. It was a brand-new recognition, never before heard or thought. Out of my struggle with resistance to fund-raising it suddenly dawned on me that of all the money I had spent on myself, I'd like tons of it back. There were shirts and shoes and ties and "stuff" that I scarcely used, some of it I actually loathed. And there were a couple of cars that quickly disenchanted me, one of them turning me quite sour and another, an antique Model A Ford, that cost an ugly bundle of money to repair and main-tain until I found another sucker to haul it away at far less cost than I had paid for it. In sum, there were whole checking accounts spent on Bennett that I would love to have back. But money that I had spent on my children, on their schools and colleges and mine, on their mother and our church and our family in those precious years—not a nickel of that did I want back, not a dime, not the warehouse of cash that I had spent on others and given away over the years. What a recognition! Suddenly it became clear to me that the human soul is much more built to give than to get, amazingly *just like Scripture says!* From then on I have believed that when you ask people for money, you are doing them a favor—whether they think so or not, or whether they give you a brass far-thing or not. Asking people for money is knocking on their secret door of freedom and joy. God is the great giver who makes all this come true. Made as we are in God's image, what fulfills God is sure to fulfill us.

After reading Bob Greenleaf's essay, I was moved to get in touch with him. I found his telephone number in the village of Peterboro, New Hampshire. I asked him to come to the diocese as leader for a clergy conference. He agreed, and a personal friendship took root and blos-somed. The diocesan clergy conference was an annual assembly involving nearly every priest and deacon in an overnight at our camp and conference center. Bob sat down in a large triple-row semicircle of chairs and just talked — and listened. He was a smash. The event made it far easier thereafter to recruit the clergy for cluster seminars of interactive learning. Bob and I kept in touch through all the years that followed until his death in 1990, largely by exchanging each other's writings.

After ten years as bishop, I hooked up with the Candler School of Theology at Emory University and taught a course in theology as a visiting lecturer. One of the most learned priests of the diocese, Charles "Ted" Hackett, served full time as a professor at Candler with special expertise in pastoral psychology. In 1979 Ted and I teamed up to invent an enterprise that would test the suitability for advancement to the seminary of the many young people who came to me in the course of every year with aspirations for the ordained ministry. We dubbed it Experiment in Ministry (EIM) and started it with nearly a dozen hopeful women and men. It was highly successful in helping people measure their desires for ordination against the realities of actual ministry. On average, about 50 percent of the aspirants qualified for the seminary. There were disappointments in the cases of those who felt misjudged, and there may well have been misjudgments, but most of those who did not qualify said that they were actually well served. However, in one particular case the ten-month experiment ended in a painful and prolonged disaster.

A thirty-something-year-old woman of outstanding intellect, who held a Ph.D., was already certified as a postulant for the first level of qualification for ordination. Next is the seminary admission level of the candidate. In the course of ten months this gifted woman had raised some questions in the minds of her peers about her readiness for candidacy. Eventually she was asked by Ted as director and by the evaluating committee to postpone advancement for a season in order to be in deeper discernment of her call. Without the slightest warning she exploded in accusatory rage, bewildering the committee and threatening a lawsuit for breach of contract and defamation of character. True to her threat, the lawsuit was filed. I was named as principal defendant, along with the suffragan bishop, the chair of the evaluation committee, and the Diocese of Atlanta as the nonprofit corporation of responsibility. She sought $5 million in damages and engaged an aggressive pro-feminist attorney, who began trying the case in the Atlanta papers. Our lawyers persuaded the court to quash the use of the media, but the succeeding year was a time of tedious depositions and occasional angry insinuations. The circuit court finally judged the case in our favor, but the plaintiff took her case to the next level of appeal. Another two years went by until the appellate court judged the case as having no merit, deciding again in our favor.

That was the end of it, but not quite. In 2003, twenty-two years after the appellate court closed the case, that gifted plaintiff tracked me down with a warm and friendly letter of salute for changing my position on same-sex orientation. She apparently did not know until more than twenty years after the fact that I had reissued a pastoral letter in 1984 changing my earlier position on the ethics of homosexuality. Still, delay in an experience of reconciliation cannot annul the deep-running joy of restoration to the oneness that human freedom presupposes as its highest expression in love. The old yearlong EIM suitability testing arrangement remains in place, although it is now called the Vocational Testing Program. We may have lost count of the number of men and women who have gone to seminaries across the country and overseas as graduates of the program, but I have yet to encounter one of them who thinks that their year of testing for ministry was a waste of time.

OUT OF THAT DEEPENING RELATIONSHIP with academia from 1979 to 1983 my desire to return to the role of seminary teacher grew apace, and I quietly began to design a new educational enterprise that I wanted to lead when I retired as bishop of Atlanta. It would take the shape of five-day interactive learning seminars for managers in all kinds of institutions, profit and nonprofit, including business, government, education, foundations, public administration, and the church. In many conversations with Jim Waits, dean of theology, and occasionally with Emory's president, James Laney, we fashioned a lively dream to create and fund a new thing in higher education. We called it the Institute for Servant Leadership, planning to link the resources of Emory's Graduate School of Business and the Candler School of Theology. The dean of the business school was George "Chip" Parks, an Episcopal layman. Chip responded warmly to the idea.

These ambitions were further stimulated by the co-incidence of my desire to advocate a Servant style of leadership with the coming of the Reagan years of American presidential philosophy. Ronald Reagan succeeded Jimmy Carter, with whom I greatly resonated for reasons of President Carter's evident, although not adequately popular, Servant approach to presidential management. Reagan, as opposed to Carter, brought an almost antithetical conceptual bias to the presidency. Under Carter, U.S. foreign policy turned toward diplomacy in facing the threat of the cold war. Under Reagan we mounted a militarily confrontational challenge. These two presidencies clearly typify the contrast between creative and conventional concepts of leadership. It is further clear that the conventional or imperial style, even in a democracy, is far more readily favored and applauded. Ronald Reagan has a major airport named for him. So too does George H. W. Bush in Houston. Not so Jimmy Carter. What this means is that leadership can be broadly understood as falling into two almost diametrically opposed conceptual categories. One can be called unilateral, the top-down, tight-box command style. The contrasting style, only now emerging slowly in leadership and management theory, is often called relational.

The unilateral mode of management assumes a triangular shape of a singular head at the peak and a descending arrangement of ancillary command and compliance—all this with a minimum of feedback loops that tend to be structurally omitted. The contrasting relational approach takes roughly the shape of a circular network, with the leader as the focus of shared authority and responsive to the automatic feedback loops that are part of the structure of the arrangement. William L.

Ury contrasts the two models in a vivid sentence: "Pyramids are held together by coercion; networks are held together by mutual consent."[2]

The Institute for Servant Leadership that I wanted to put in place at Emory would be cast forthrightly in the relational mode. While the relational mode is beginning to reshape the character of American management, the long-standing imperial or pyramid model remains heavily popular. One of the most admired CEOs in recent times, former General Electric head Jack Welch, defined his leadership style as "kicking butt and hugging." Notice that the "kick"; takes precedence over the "hug." This is what I would call a Reaganesque unilateralism. It is in high currency under the presidency of George W. Bush and his administration. This is true especially in the Department of Defense under Donald Rumsfeld and in the Department of Justice under super-patriot John Ashcroft. The brash unilateralism of present American leadership was betrayed most clearly in the administration's rush to war in Iraq in scorn of the United Nations Security Council and the outcry of marching millions at home and around the world. It remains to be seen whether a carefully orchestrated fear-and-fury arousal in the American electorate will return this unilateralism to power in the next election.

MY RETIREMENT PROCESS as bishop climaxed in late 1983 and included a large banquet in that same cathedral hall that welcomed me into office almost twelve years earlier. The splendid party also included a handsome gift check for almost $30,000. Excited to be at work again as a teacher, I went to Emory University as an adjunct professor in the Candler School of Theology. My wife and I had purchased our own home in Atlanta by then, a condominium near Emory. All the while we kept our winterized and considerably upgraded cottage on the lake in Eagles Mere, Pennsylvania. Our marriage, though deeply troubled, was still marked by hopeful tenderness, and we looked forward to long summers at the mountain house and eventual full retirement there. I was sixty-three, in good health, and full of ginger for teaching and fund-raising as director of the new and experimental Institute for Servant Leadership. Jim Waits had secured foundation funding for launching the enterprise, and the school awarded me the salary of a full professor.

Bob Greenleaf was much involved. A year earlier, while still bishop, I had invited him to Atlanta for a day of "blueprinting" the institute, scheduled to start up the following academic year. In addition to Bob and me, the design committee included the president of Emory, the deans of the theology and business schools, and three prominent businesspeople in Atlanta. We met for a long day and agreed on several guiding principles. First, the institute would involve only those in leadership roles at any level, in a variety of institutional settings. Second, participants would include both women and men. Third, the learning setting would be circular, with lectures balanced by casework for interactive sharing. Fourth, the time frame would be a five-day residential retreat venue in a conference center near Atlanta. Fifth, informal worship and brief scriptural meditations would be a voluntary offering at the beginning of each day. Sixth, at least three or four such five-day seminars

would span the academic year, with a return conference for follow-up at least every other year. From the
start we wanted Jimmy Carter to be the principal in the
first of those return conferences. The former president
was already on the adjunct faculty of Emory and carried a reputation for world leadership as a spiritually
grounded public servant. President Carter did lead our
first return conference, and over one hundred of our
alumni attended from many parts of the nation.

The only wrinkle in the previously described day-
long planning session with Bob Greenleaf was his grim
forecast that the whole thing would never survive.
From his long experience in researching and advocat-
ing this style of leading institutions, he said that Servant
Leadership was the most applauded and least practiced management philosophy in America, and that the
churches, of all institutions, were the most guilty of ideo-
logical agreement and practical refusal. But he did wish
us good luck! After the institute had been in business for
about four years, in an undulating pattern of flying and
faltering, and before his death, Bob did cheerfully salute
us. The last time we were together was at a service in
Washington for the inaugural of the Servant Leadership
School of the Church of the Savior. Bob had to be helped
up from his chair for the honor accorded him, and he
died within months at age eighty-six. Our institute remains in vigorous life with a constituency of alumni
that spans the nation and reaches into distant places
around the world. The most recent use of my 1997 book
Servanthood was with a conference of twenty bishops
of the Anglican province of Tanzania, in May 2003. I
was invited to be the conference leader but could not for

reasons of age and limited strength. My friends Bishop Herbert Donovan and his scholarly wife, Mary, took the assignment. The local bishop and my new friend Simon Chiwanga, wrote that the event was a great success.

BEFORE RETIREMENT AS BISHOP and starting up the Institute for Servant Leadership, I broke silence about my hopes for a return to teaching with only a few people, and always with a request for confidentiality. First, after my wife, was the Reverend Newton Gordon Cosby, renowned and beloved minister of the vigorous outreaching and ecumenical Church of the Savior in Washington, D.C. Years before, Gordon and I had developed a close friendship that spanned the Potomac for the six years of my work at the Virginia Seminary, and our friendship extended into my years as bishop of Atlanta. I was already deep into connections with Emory, though not yet thinking out loud about leaving the office of bishop to start a new enterprise at the university. But the idea was alive and bubbling. I had asked Gordon to come as our clergy conference leader in the spring of 1982. He allowed as how he seldom did this sort of thing, but in light of our long association, he would come. He did, and like Bob Greenleaf before him by several years, Gordon was a smash. Biblically learned, deeply disciplined in spirit, and rigorously committed to the worldly Christ of human toil and suffering, Gordon is a luminous man of God. Following the conference, I drove him the two-hour trip back to the Atlanta airport and felt moved to share with him my dream of an institute at Emory. Expecting him to be wisely circumspect in reply, asking questions, probing my purpose, and suggesting impediments, I was astounded when his first response was, "Do it!" As for the probing and the purpose and the impediments, I was the one to talk about these things, in the midst of which he said again, "Just do it." From one who had made a ministry on the frontier of Christian innovation for years—and with resounding results—I felt girded as if by God to go forth and "get at it." And so it came to be.

In December 1983, a few weeks before my official retirement from the bishop's office, we convened the institute's opening seminar at the Unicoi Conference Center in north Georgia, about an hour's drive from Atlanta. Unicoi is a state facility, beautifully rustic and amply furnished with every convenience for learning and community building. The conference center was a special project of Jimmy Carter's when he served as governor of Georgia in the 1970s. About fifteen women and men from a wide variety of institutional leadership had signed on. They were educators, business leaders, physicians, public administrators, and clergy. The teachers on staff were four plus Dr. Barbara Wheeler, dean of Auburn Seminary in New York, as evaluator for Emory University. The four instructors were James W. Rouse, founder of the Rouse Company of Columbia, Maryland, developers of the new city of Columbia and later founder of the Enterprise Foundation for low-cost housing in cities across America; an old teaching colleague from Virginia Seminary days, Dr. James H. Laue, now become professor of sociology at Washington University in St. Louis; Thomas Dolgoff, a gifted industrial psychologist from the Menninger Foundation; and myself as theologian. All but Dr. Wheeler and I are now deceased.

In addition to teaching, recruiting, and fund-raising I began a periodic newsletter that soon became a quarterly and then a bimonthly piece which we named *Turning Point.* It was mailed to all alumni of the Institute for Servant Leadership and to all whom we hoped to recruit for later seminars. My favorite of all the early *Turning Points* is the winter issue of 1987. It constitutes a ringing challenge to the "great god of Competition" as a delusional idol with the sinister power to undermine the health of the human spirit. I titled it "Competition: Friend or Foe of Self-Esteem?"[3]

One of the easiest things to sell from an airport book rack would be a paperback emblazoned with a big $ sign and called "How to Beat the Competition." Such items are already out there with a variety of come-on titles. America is addicted to competition.

My earliest remembered competitive reward system goes back to the second grade. The teacher was Miss Bonney, no doubt trained herself to bow before the great god of competition. She was a kind but cunning child-motivator. She divided the class into three groups: Bluebirds, Busy Bees and Fireflies — all fairly innocuous words to soften the impact of what she had in mind. But there was no softening the impact of being assigned to group three. If you were a Firefly you were a classroom drag unless you could drag yourself to the next level. Chester Funk (his real name) was a Firefly. He never spoke. I remember him as a sort of broken boy who took no part in recess games or class mischief. There were probably others in and out of the Fireflies whom I don't remember with pain. They may have been better protected in spirit than Chester who had not an ounce of bully belligerence.

Of course, Miss Bonney's purpose was to get us to fly with the Bluebirds as quick learners and cooperative little girls and boys. But a powerful counterproductivity was constantly at work. The system made it impossible for all but a favored few to be Bluebirds since we were pitted against standards subtly set by the lead group itself. The effect of this was to pit the children against each other. Thus the question: How can Miss Bonney's own ideal of cooperation be taught by a mechanism that defines collaboration as cheating?

Only once did I make it to the Bluebird table. For a couple of weeks I basked in the company of Lester Fellner, who was born with a computer under his unruly red hair, and with Rose Schaufman, who could recite verses as if she had written them for breakfast. Lots of us from the Busy Bee table (the largest group) graduated from the second grade convinced we were lame-brained but still favored for not having to stagger shamefully into third grade as Fireflies — or, God forbid, having to repeat the ignominy of second grade!

It took years as a certified Busy Bee to discover three things that lifted my self-appreciation. First, personal worth has little to do with IQ. I found friends later with scores that blew the top of the IQ chart but who struggled quite as much, or more, as I did with self-esteem. Second, it was anxiety, deep-seated dread, and not inferior native ability that kept me from the company of Lester and Rose. (Looking back, I think I grew up scared.) Third, human endeavor, when keenly understood, relies best on a deep spiritual preference for collaboration over competition.

It may be hard to sell Lee Iacocoa on this last point, but that fierce competitor actually relied on the truth of it to get Chrysler out of the doldrums. Most conspicuously he succeeded in making collaborators out of adversaries when the

unions and management agreed that jobs were more valu-
able than a particular pay scale. Just to work, just to have
productive employment proves fundamental to self-esteem.
The desire to be productive runs deeper than the drive for
pay. Research in 1982 showed that 75 percent of American
nonmanagement work force felt it was under-employed and
wanted greater personal challenge on the job.[4]

These results prompted more research in business circles.
Robert Helmreich of the University of Texas discovered an
inverse relationship between competitiveness and achieve-
ment: salaries go up as competitiveness goes down. All the
research cited in the article suggests that "trying to beat
others" and "trying to do well" are two very different things;
they actually work at cross-purposes. The reason for this is
clear: in cooperative situations others are depending on
each person to succeed; in competitive situations others
hope to see you fail.

Back to the Bluebirds, Busy Bees and Fireflies. The late
renowned educator John Holt had some astringent words for
Miss Bonney. He said that we destroy the love of learning in
children, which is so strong when they are small, by com-
pelling them to work for petty and contemptible rewards—
gold stars, or papers marked 100 and tacked to the wall... or
deans' lists, or Phi Beta Kappa keys—in short, for the igno-
ble satisfaction that they are better than someone else. The
truth of humanity is that no one is better than anyone else.
Any system that seeks to differentiate people on the basis
of superior/inferior personal worth is bound to fail. And it
fails thunderously in the marketplace where it not only cuts
productivity but encourages greed, rapacity, lying, cheating
and gross social inequities that afflict our national spirit and

rob us of the inner rewards that ought to be ours in a free and affluent society.

C. G. Jung held that competitive self-assertion is useful for ego development in the first half of life, but that a shift into a new mode needs to occur somewhere along the line that moves between the ego and what he called the Self. I may have misinterpreted Jung in this analysis, but if my impressions are correct, and in all due respect to Jung's surpassing genius, I think he is wrong here. John Holt's testimony would argue precisely the reverse. My sense is that competition and collaboration go together simultaneously, not as separated time sequences. They relate concurrently from beginning to end as action (competition) and arena (collaboration)—as spice and substance. Competition is salt and pepper. Collaboration is meat and potatoes. The great affliction of our culture is that we have been feeding ourselves on the condiments of salt and pepper while starving our souls for want of the real food of life. The most recent research into human behavior, both modern and prehistoric (as with the hunter-gatherer societies of primitive African and South American tribal people), begins to draw a clear profile of genetically programmed preference for collaboration over competition. What this means is that competition is a friend of self-esteem only when set in the context of collaboration, as in a team effort. *Without a supportive and personally valuing framework, competition becomes* violence *and the human spirit never knows its worth, either one's own self-worth or that of others.*

Servant Leadership is a quality of attention to persons that values the spice of competition while insisting on an arena, by which I mean a community, for giving and receiving the variety of gifts of human energy—in the family, the school, the workplace and in the compressing world of interwoven human belonging. If this deduction is to be trusted, then Servant Leadership becomes indispensable to the health and survival of the whole human odyssey.

This was written sixteen years ago, and, though it seems up-to-date in one sense, in light of the historical research that forms the content of Chapter Six in this book, Jung's analysis is a bull's eye when set in the corporate context of the long evolving human species story covering about 100,000 years. Whatever time frame is assigned, individual or species development, it means that in a world threatened by American first-strike nuclear privilege and "blazing competition for dominion," Servant Leaders are the people who can pull the world back to sanity — back from the teetering brink of weaponized self-destruction under bellicose unilateral American leadership.

Chapter Three

Leadership as
the Exercise of Power

*Power is like love. It is one of those precious things that
grows by giving it away.*

—Rosabeth Moss Kanter, Harvard Business School

THE INSTITUTE FOR SERVANT LEADERSHIP at the
School of Theology of Emory University was begun
with a partnership between the institute and the university's School of Business Administration. The reason for
this is the plain truth of the overwhelming power and
presence of business and industry in the institutional
life of America and all of Western-shaped world culture.
If the institute was going to "speak truth to power," we
had to find ways into the hearts and minds of business
leadership. The narrow but highly significant common
ground for the graduate schools of business and theology was that both were educating leaders in two
splendid but unlinked academic institutions.

My question in those early days was how to con-
ceptualize a partnership between a discipline devoted
primarily to getting and another committed presumably to giving. Of course, the reality is that both business
and religion are eagerly into both activities. Business

must give in order to get. Products come with warranties, and services must be offered with a smile. As for the church, with its salaried hierarchies and tall steeples, ecclesiastical establishments must get in order to give. As an ordained clergyperson in a wide variety of assignments, I have had to be a fund-raiser for more than half a century. Facing the need to raise three quarters of a million dollars in the late 1950s to build a new church and related buildings in Baltimore, my canny senior warden, Dr. Huntington Williams, cautioned me about being too optimistic. "Remember," he said, "for Episcopalians, money isn't everything, but whatever is in second place is a long way behind!" The fact that we met the goal made a cryptic joke of the senior warden's comment, and Dr. Williams knew it. Deep down, while the lure of money is a corrupting lust, the human spirit knows the higher power of a commanding love.

My critical problem in launching the institute was to find a way to define leadership in such a way as to bridge the conceptual and practical gaps between "for profit" and "not for profit" leadership, how to harmonize an understanding of leadership that could bring a sense of inner unity and wholeness to the minds and souls of leaders in all kinds of institutions so that they could be the same persons in all settings — whether it be at the office on Monday or in church on Sunday. We conducted seminars and conferences for a couple of years without a clear answer to the question of wholeness of heart for leaders in disparate institutions. Then in one intuitive moment, when "something crossed my path" (as Carl Jung or Robert Frost might say of an unbeckoned gift of the spirit), it struck me that *all leadership is the exercise of power.*

From parenting to presiding, from the family house to the White House, all leaders use power. But there is a terrific problem in using the word *power.* Almost never does it carry a servant connotation. Just the reverse. In both the dictionary and in popular parlance *power* means "dominance." *Webster's* defines power as "control," "subjugation," and "the capacity to compel compliance." This is exactly what we mean by the word *Superpower,* and this is exactly how the United States is exercising power in expanding our military dominance as we stride across the world. At the expense of manifest needs in education, health care, and environmental controls, we are busy spending our substance on the capacity to compel compliance with subjugational force.

But if we go from the dictionary and politics to the New Testament and look closely at one of history's undisputed great leaders, a more profound, more enduring form of power emerges. At every turn in the record of his work Jesus of Nazareth used power for a quite different purpose than dominance. History since then has underlined the paradox that, while Jesus did not aim to dominate, his life and death and continuing life have become dominant in defining the spiritual and ethical odyssey of Western culture. The same paradox applies to the Buddha whose life and teaching have shaped the character of human values in the Asian world ever since he forsook the dominant privileges of princely birth for the simplicity of a nonviolent love and regard for all forms of sentient life.

In essence, what we are looking at in the lives of Jesus and the Buddha is the power, not to dominate, but to make a difference. *To make a difference.* That is the true meaning of power, and the best thing about true power is that everybody has it. Power in its deepest and most enduring terms is every person's gift — from womb to tomb and well beyond. Power in the womb is exercised by every life who is expected. That expectation runs the gamut of sensations, including joy, foreboding, wonder, anxiety, and outright rejection. This power is both private and public. In the womb its privacy is in a pregnant mother's intensely personal response. In public its power lies in the intensity of political contention between the forces of pro-life and pro-choice. Returning to the tomb, its public power lies in the levels of esteem and disesteem of all who hold anyone in memory. Public tomb power is exemplified by history's heroines and heroes, and equally by history's hooligans.

SOON AFTER NATHAN PUSEY was installed as Harvard University's new president, his wife, Anne, was invited as a guest of honor to a fashionable tea at the Beacon Hill home of a Boston socialite. Mrs. Pusey, impressed with the variety of lovely hats in the circle of guests, was moved to ask her hostess, "Tell me, where do your friends get their stunning hats?" Quickly came the answer, "Oh, my dear, in Boston we don't get hats; we *have* them!" Just so in the case of every human being: at the base of life we don't *get* power, we *have* it. All forms of life, including the lower forms, have power by virtue of the gift of life itself. The question for us humans, as the higher and self-conscious expression of life, is therefore not whether we have power, but *how shall power be used?*

I HAVE COME TO UNDERSTAND all temptation in terms of this very question, since presumably only human beings possess the moral freedom to be tempted. How shall I use my power? This is the question that goes to the heart of personal freedom and to all human constructs of governance. The classic saga of temptation is in the very private experience of Jesus of Nazareth. As reported in both Matthew and Luke, it is so private an experience that it can only have gotten into the record by virtue of a personal disclosure by Jesus himself. That he chose to tell about this deeply personal confrontation with the choice of how to use his power must mean that it was of capital significance to Jesus. It stands at the headwaters of the ever-flowing river of his teaching.

There are three highly symbolic thrusts of the Tempter to use personal power for either dominance or for what I want to name "Servanthood." These three are in both Matthew and Luke, but in different sequences. Using the sequence in the version in Matthew, the *first* lure is to exercise dominance over nature. Jesus staggered with hunger after a lengthy fast, making him extremely vulnerable to the challenge "Turn these stones to bread." Whether or not he really could have done this is not the question. All three temptations are symbolic of human capability, and in our time we know the immensely critical character of human power over the natural order. If contemporary human power to dominate and exploit the natural order goes unchecked, the planet must perish as the resource base for all of life. Jesus's answer takes the challenge up to a higher level than bodily craving. His answer defines the enduring hungers of the human heart, the hungers that no feasting on food can ever slake: "One does not live by bread alone, but by every word that comes from the mouth of God."[1] Jesus does not deny bodily hunger; he simply elevates human need to the level of soul. That is where real power resides: in choices of the soul where decisions about the use of true power are made, whether to dominate, subjugate, exploit, or serve. Albert Schweitzer lived the truth of Servanthood as a choice open to all. He wrote, "The only ones among you who will be truly happy are those who have sought and found how to serve." That Jesus chose the road of Servant power is clear from his public life and from his response to the second temptation.

The *second* address to the lure of dominant power moves from relationship to the natural order to relationship with one's interpersonal network to relationship with family, neighbors, circles of friends, and associates and subordinates in the workplace. "The devil then took him to the Holy City and set him on the parapet of the temple. 'If you are the son of God,' he said, 'throw yourself down; for Scripture says, "He will put his angels in charge of you, and they will support you in their arms. . . ." ' "[2] In effect this is a summons to bedazzle the crowd with the miraculous, using power to subjugate others to one's will. But in terms of both Scripture and real life, this is not miraculous. It is magic, and magic requires secrecy, sleight of hand, and a practiced skill in fooling the public. The miracles of Jesus are never in the dark, never for the purpose of dominance or exploitation. Some reported miracles, like walking on water and stilling a storm, look like editorial additions by the writers in the early believing community when the record of Jesus's ministry was transmitted orally and not written as Gospels for another generation or more after his death. Such reported occasions are most likely exaggerations characteristic of literature that seeks to commend and exalt history's high heroes. In those "fictional" cases, it is important to be clear that they were done in service to others, *not for self-aggrandizing dominance.* Also, it is important to keep in mind that most of the reported miracles are in service to health and normalcy. They never take the normal and convert it to the abnormal. Jesus never makes gold of goldfish or compels cows to jump over the moon. Even in reports that he raised the dead, his action was to convert the abnormal to the normal. It is not normal for a twelve-year-old girl to die or a widow's son to go early to the grave. No doubt the early believing community remembered and orally embellished the memory of Jesus, but it is important to recognize that not one of the reported miracles is performed in terms of the Tempter's seduction to use power for subjugation, bedazzlement, or manipulation. *Every miracle, whether real, embellished, or invented, fits precisely the high norms of Servanthood.*

The convincing miracles seize the disordered and restore order. The lame walk, the deaf hear, the blind see, the hungry are fed, the diseased are made whole, and the possessed are repossessed of their composure. This is Servant power. It exalts others, not the self. Servant power is recognizable by its fruits, and its chief fruit is that it makes others powerful. Servant power calls forth the powers implicit in the gift of life. Servant power forces nothing. It implants nothing. It works by evocation of what is already there, seeing intended wholeness in what appears only partial or unsummoned. This is the power that must have turned Simon bar Jonah, the courtyard coward on a Thursday night, to Peter the Rock fifty days later when, on Pentecost, he boldly confronted any such persons in the Jerusalem festival crowd who had acquiesced in the bloody murder of the crucified. This is evocation, not manipulation. This must be the meaning of Jesus's reply to the Tempter when he returned the challenge by refusing to "tempt God" — refusing to do tricks and manipulate reality. The manipulation of reality is not power. It is weakness, as all lying and distortions of the truth are capitulations to weakness. Lying sets the seal on its own demise because it violates the character of the cosmos ruled by its Creator in truth and self-giving love. This underlines a distinctive theological truth: that God in the revelation of Jesus is not a divine dominator, not a manipulator, and never a high-and-mighty self-serving subjugator. In the crystal image of Jesus as the face of God in history, the Ruler of the universe is supreme in the exercise of Servant power.

> Here is God: no monarch he,
> throned in easy state to reign;
> Here is God whose arms of love,
> aching, spent, the world sustain.[3]

The *third* lure is to empire building, perhaps the most pernicious and fatal of all temptations open to human choice. Surely it is the most public and the most open to the inevitability of violence, injustice, and tyranny.

The Tempter took Jesus to a panoramic view of all the kingdoms of the world. "All these I will give you," he said to Jesus, "if you will fall down and worship me."[4] Capitulation to this lure must be what Lord Acton had in mind in laying down the axiom "Power tends to corrupt, and absolute power corrupts absolutely." What he refers to is clearly the dominating and controlling force of power, in popular and dictionary terms. We know that this is the subjugating power he had in mind, because of our attribution to God as absolute in power while trusting divine power to be anything but corrupt. The prayerful address to "*Almighty* God" is a statement of trust in the absolute incorruptibility of divinity. This theological certainty is warrant for attributing to God the primary power of divine Servanthood as revealed in the life, death, and continuing life of Jesus.

As I CONTEND ELSEWHERE in this personal and political odyssey, history is uniformly unkind to empires. They appear to have erupted into human formations of dominant power 7,000 to 5,000 years ago and later with the appearance of Egypt, Sumer, Persia, Babylon, and others, in their train. All are now gone save for Communist China, in its takeover of Tibet, and the United States, in our contemporary lust for using dominant power to force "regime changes" in a variety of nations. American imperialism may have begun rather modestly when President Theodore Roosevelt authorized the occupation of Nicaragua, the Dominican Republic, and Haiti soon after the Spanish-American War. It reached noteworthy proportions on August 19, 1953, when Kermit Roosevelt, grandson of Teddy and an operative of the Central Intelligence Agency, orchestrated the ouster of Mohammed Mossadegh, then the Iranian prime minister. Mossadegh was a populist leader who had aroused the wrath of the British by nationalizing the British-owned oil industry. He also had frightened Washington by failing to oppose Communist influence inside Iran. Now, in 2004, American imperialism runs in high gear with the use of dominant military force to engineer regime changes in the Middle East—all with lively hints of moving this imperial power into other nations on the "axis of evil." The temptation to imperialism remains both powerful and fatal. History is not mocked. Empires fail.

This is not to suggest that dominant power is fundamentally bad or never applicable. All leaders set boundaries. These are the acceptable parameters of behavior, established for the good of both the leaders and the led. Everyone in a leadership role sets boundaries. This makes boundary setting itself a form of Servanthood. Mothers are good at this: "Get your elbows off the table." Bosses set boundaries: "Get to work on time." So do teachers: "Do the reading, and get to class." Jesus did likewise: "...those who want to save their life will lose it, and those who lose their life for my sake and for the sake, of the gospel, will save it."[5] Jesus capsulized God's own boundary setting in answering a religious lawyer's query about how he might inherit eternal life. Interestingly, Jesus said nothing about sexual behavior, be it hetero- or homosexual. Evil must have been rooted for Jesus somewhere else than in sex, but not for most of the Christian tradition since St. Augustine invented the doctrine of original sin. That, it seems to me, rose from

Augustine's own personal shame in sexual adventuring as a young man. From that guilty memory he appears to have hit upon the idea that the Evil, to which we all capitulate, springs originally from Adam's lust for sexual intercourse with Eve. This doctrine, peculiar to Christianity, is nowhere in Scripture and was historically impossible to have lodged in the high moral consciousness of Jesus. Jesus, after all, precedes Augustine in time by three centuries!

In answer to the lawyer's query, Jesus simply asked the man to answer his own question from an ecclesiastical lawyer's professional knowledge of the Hebrew tradition. The lawyer quickly repeated the biblical summary: "You shall love the Lord your God with all your heart, and with all your soul, and with all your strength, and with all your mind; and your neighbor as yourself." Jesus nodded approval and said: "Do this and you will live."[6] Earlier in the history of Christian writing than the Gospels, a convert from the elaborate rigidity of Hebrew rule making wrote, "Owe no one anything, except to love one another.... Love does no wrong to a neighbor; therefore love is the fulfilling of the law."[7] Behold the paradox of real power. Love and law go together to complete the meaning of Servanthood. This is the balance of velvet and steel in all expressions of servant leadership. Or to put it differently, there is no real Servanthood without the service of boundaries.

I AM FASCINATED by a horse trainer who works with this mystic balance of velvet and steel. His name is Monty Roberts, and he is famous as the "Horse Whisperer." He does not use the force of whip and bronco-busting dominance. He does not "break" a horse's will under the superior force of a rider from "on top" while the horse bucks and snorts and tears the turf. Roberts uses the mystic balance of iron and eiderdown to "tame" a horse to an experience of controlled horsepower. The iron in his taming process is a rope, a long restraining leash. His use of eye-to-eye contact is the eiderdown in his method. In the taming process he never rides the horse from a coercive position "on top." He is "on the level," in a posture of relational equality. He gets inside the horse with his sense of kinship with the animal. Taming for Roberts is a soul-to-soul exercise, using the rope and walking the horse in a slow circle while trusting the mystic connection between the leader and the led. In twenty to thirty minutes the horse, without resistance, will receive a bit and bridle and a blanket and saddle— ready for riding or racing or pulling in the traces. The Horse Whisperer, as the horse's servant leader, releases the already present horse power for the animal's own servanthood.

Monty Roberts uses a long loop of rope as a rein. *But the rope is never a weapon.* It is a tool, an implement for beginning the process of trusting a horse into a voluntary claim on horse power. It is a leash for letting loose the coiled forces of body and soul that are native to the horse. Its message is "Be not afraid. I love you." As for religion, we need to be wary of any theology that uses the Bible as more than a leash, a leash for letting loose our created human powers. Beware of a "biblicism" that wields the Bible as a weapon, playing upon and compounding our fear. Much of that abounds these days.

From a tragic misreading of the Bible through the distorting lens of fundamentalist literalism, it supports the violence of war and clings to the injustice of denying the full humanity of gay and lesbian persons who are made so by endowments of sexual identity in the womb. In scorn of the character of divine power as proclaimed in Jesus, fundamentalism perpetuates the male-dominant paradigm that perceives power as dominance.

VIOLENCE IS THE CAPITAL DIFFERENCE between dominant and Servant power. Dominance always carries with it an implied or explicit threat. Dominance either whispers or shouts "Do this or else." What it means is "Be afraid." By contrast, Servanthood is explicitly nonviolent and seeks to eliminate fear in the manner of the velvet and steel of Jesus of Nazareth:

> Peace I leave with you; my peace I give you. I do not give to you as the world gives. Do not let your hearts be troubled, and do not let them be afraid.[8]

IT IS CRITICALLY IMPORTANT to American freedom and to the nation's collaborative capacities that there be mounted a vigorous contending political force in the forthcoming election. The secret for defeating the self-defeating lust for empire and the self-righteous scorn of other nations is to *get the voting public to the polls.* Trustworthy recent research shows that current political leanings, if energized, can remove the menacing incumbent administration. Only 30 percent of Americans claim a sharply conservative political preference. The 70 percent balance divides as 50 percent moderate and 20 percent liberal. The winning strategy is clear: *mobilize the moderate middle.* Without such a surge, the present self-serving contempt of other nations and cultures must ultimately bring resounding defeat to an America enamored of its own subjugating power. This is the clarion call of history. All the empires of human emergence since 5000 BCE are dead and gone save for China and ourselves, and they and we will not be exempted from the dynamics of imperial birth and death. Empires are born in the lust of dominant power, and they die by the abiding force of the relational power that fashioned a Cross of compassion and servanthood — and brought an Easter of triumph for the self-giving forces of God that birthed the cosmos and spins the bountiful earth around our star.

Important as it is to replace the imperial takeover of President Bush and company, and important as it is to mobilize the electorate for an American "regime change," of greater importance for the long-term hope of America is the rise of another superpower in the world community. The world's resounding popular resistance to the Iraqi war looks like greatly added energy for turning the massive hinge of history on which the world now moves pulling humanity up from a long adolescent addiction to the violence of dominant power to the maturity of nonviolent relational equality in a new global civilization. This phenomenon seems to me clearly a fresh power up from the depths of our collective unconscious, born of a new certainty that at this juncture of history the violence of the ages has reached such a pitch of lethal menace that, facing the possible incineration of our home base in the cosmos, we must either grow up or blow up.

Instantly this means that Servant power has moved from option to necessity. It makes a mission in Servant Leadership fit hand in glove with the emergence across the world of an advancing momentum of the healing power in nonviolent resolutions of conflict. Extinction is a continuous exercise in the long, long emergence of life on the planet, and the human species may be calling down that same ineluctable engine of evolution in our nuclear capacity to incinerate the world. But there is a counterengine that throbs with increasing muscle in the rising tide of commitment to a Servant posture in personal and institutional leadership. Human extinction, along with the loss of much of the planet's life, may yet be forestalled. A world imperiled by the lust and swagger of a bloated political power now cries out for a rapid increase in the numbers and self-giving energy of Servant Leaders. On both sides of the present political contention, Republican and Democrat, there lives a deep and sturdy wish that life for ourselves and for our children's children will continue. *To the extent that such a wish is incontestable, then Servanthood appears the only way open to a human future.*

Chapter Four

Apocalypse and Evolution

I refuse to accept the view that mankind is so tragically bound to the starless midnight of racism and war that the bright daybreak of peace and brotherhood can never become a reality.... I believe that unarmed truth and unconditional love will have the final word.

—Martin Luther King Jr.

THE SEPTEMBER 11, 2001, terrorist attack on New York's World Trade Center produced two widely different political reactions. One was unexceptional, the other quite astonishing. The first reaction was to be expected. Retaliate! Make war. Revenge the wickedness. Use military force to bring terrorism to heel. The result was an instant forest of flags and an epidemic outbreak of patriotic slogans on bumper stickers. The presidential mantra filled the airwaves: God bless America! A major hidden meaning in this popular rash of revenge represents what was written in an earlier chapter identifying Carl Jung's theory of projection. This was the analyst's name for what Jesus identified as the natural human impulse to seek to remove the splinter from an adversary's eye while being unaware of the great plank in one's own eye—for which accusatory insight and other offenses to human pride Jesus was executed.

The second response to 9/11 makes it possible to speculate that perhaps we have come a little distance from the rage that crucified Jesus for his offenses to the cultural pomp that hides the darkness in every heart. While holding some of Jung's deductions in doubt, the professional world did not crucify the great analyst. He died at age eighty-six in the world's honor. More than that, all the healing professions rely more or less heavily on his telling insights about the subversive powers of the "inner shadow" that can hold the human spirit in the grip of psychic tyranny and spiritual illness. Mario Cuomo, the former governor of New York, in an interview on the heels of the terrorist carnage of 9/11, gave voice to the other political reaction, the exceptional one. As a Roman Catholic Christian, he talked about the two things that, in his judgment, all the religions of the world advocate in their basic ethical teachings.

The first, he said, is the powerful healing impulse in the human capacity to love one another. He saw this indiscriminate caring for others operating everywhere in the self-giving, even life-sacrificing, service of firefighters, police, and the hordes of nameless helpers who rallied in support of the injured and sorrowing in the carnage of collapsing towers. The second, he said, is the call to rebuild what is broken—to heal the divisions that alienate humanity and subvert the longing for peace. What Governor Cuomo had in mind was rebinding the broken bones of lower Manhattan, but he also made reference to the brokenness in the human family that underlies the cruelty and devastation of the attack.

Had Mr. Cuomo been president, I do not know whether he would have moderated the strident call to counterviolence as American policy in response to savage terrorism. But his comments on the heels of the disaster suggest that he might have ordered a response that reflected a solemn recognition that American behavior is not without culpability in fueling the seething hatreds of fundamentalist passion. The reality is that in America we are victims of a similar fundamentalist fervor. Ours is not as grossly suicidal in personal terms, except perhaps in the case of abortion clinic bombers. But in public terms our passion may be quite suicidal. Consider that we have

1. installed an administration and a Congress that conspire to abridge constitutional freedoms in punitive patriot legislation;

2. penalized public education, health, and social security in favor of exploding deficits in support of a mammoth nuclear-backed military capability; and

3. mounted our first preemptive war and challenged the sovereignty of any nation that we deem "evil" for having unfriendly nuclear capability or that is rich in oil reserves.

Violence is the ethos of our time. It is pervasive across national and religious boundaries. It keeps the Middle East in flames, especially in the endless Israeli-Palestine exchange of murder, and it mires the world's lone superpower in economic and spiritual peril. Both the roots and the fruits of fundamentalist violence are laced with fury and dread. The distinguished theologian and researcher Karen Armstrong holds that there are many complex motives that give rise to fundamentalism, but at the base of them all is a pervasive fear. It is the fear of losing the securities of certainty, fear of losing anchorage in changeless custom, all of it compounding a self-protective blindness to any culpability for failed and broken relationships.

Fear is everybody's lurking enemy. It is the destroyer of both personal and interpersonal peace. This makes everybody a candidate for some degree of fundamentalist fervor. But a healthy soul knows the enemy's name and its alienating power, and is able to summon detachment from the pernicious impulse to assign all blame outward in fear and accusation. For the Muslims who flew the assault planes on 9/11, their bizarre expectation of reward in heaven obviously overrode their fear of death, while the suicide action itself betrayed another kind of fear. This other kind is the continuing fear of the world-penetrating values and secular indulgences of the United States that threaten Muslim terrorists with the loss of the security that comes of belonging to their own meaning and reward-giving religio-political system. In the United States that same fear operates to hurl our power against the attackers: we dread losing our meaning and reward-giving membership in a God-bestowed political system. And our counterfear is fed with some regularity by administration-generated warnings of imminent terrorist attacks.

MY ANALYSIS MAY BE WRONG, or at least myopic, but in my assessment of our present political policy of armed and endless violence it seems to me that the world is caught in the cross fire of rage between two opposing "jihads," two snarling and self-righteous religious fundamentalisms that feed on the illusion of "holy war." They are Islamic on one side and Christian-Zionist on the other. The two contenders seem determined on a course of mutual extermination. There is no argument that Islamic fundamentalism is embarked on a violent holy war. That is made clear by the terrorists' own propaganda. Not so clear is the American political leadership that is shaped by an apocalyptic fundamentalism. Ronald Reagan gave it credence, and George W. Bush now capitalizes on it. Riane Eisler, in her popular book *The Chalice and the Blade,* footnotes the bimonthly journal *Liberty* (November–December 1985) that quotes President Reagan as having "suggested on at least eleven occasions that the end of the world is coming."[1] This ominous apocalypticism has been restored to the White House. The vision of policy "wonks" in the administration holds that America's place and purpose in the world commits us to armed violence as a way of righteousness that brooks no critique from outside its circle of decision makers. The president has been repeatedly challenged to give ear to the moderating voices of peace-oriented religious leadership in all the major church bodies, including the pope and the Dalai Lama — all except the Southern Baptist Convention of America, which, on the whole, is committed to a fierce fundamentalist passion. The president, it will be remembered, visited and addressed Bob Jones University in Greenville, South Carolina, very early in his campaign for the presidency. Bob Jones is a proudly fundamentalist teaching powerhouse that, during the civil rights era, vilified Martin Luther King Jr. and maintained a strict segregationist policy for some time afterward.

THE PRESENT BUSH ADMINISTRATION is served by brilliant policy people who counsel armed violence as a matter of virtue. One of those closest to the president and his team is Michael Lindeen. Lindeen is quoted in the May 23, 2003, issue of the *National Catholic Reporter* as advancing violence and preemptive war as national policies: "Change, above all violent change, is the essence of human history...." *This is a patently spurious claim.* It betrays an ignorance of most of human prehistory, which archaeology and paleontology prove to have been largely nonviolent for all but a fraction of the approximately 100,000 years of sentient human presence on the planet. Supporting scientific evidence of our long nonviolent past will be laid out in the following chapter. Meanwhile, Dr. Lindeen, on the basis of severely limited historical knowledge, advocates violent American conquest. In the same article he writes, "Destruction is our middle name. We do it automatically.... It is time once again to export the democratic revolution.... The sparing of civilian lives cannot be the total war's first priority.... The purpose of total war is to permanently force your will onto another people." He proposes that a fundamentalist American policy be now focused on lands beyond Iraq: "The time for diplomacy is at an end; it is time to free Iran, free Syria and free Lebanon."[2] Fury and fear. These look like the staples of American leadership policy.

As for fear, America has been gripped by it before, but earlier leadership handled it by pledging to reduce fear, not to exacerbate it. In the depression years of my adolescence Franklin Roosevelt, acknowledging social and economic dread, addressed it directly in his inaugural challenge that our real enemy was fear itself and that the government was pledged to rally us in defeating its ugly and enervating power. By contrast now, fear mounts in a society starkly different from the one led by Roosevelt. This administration sustains a fairly steady drumbeat of warnings of further terrorist assaults, and their policy representations persist in reducing investment in legislation that lifts the burden of poverty while pressing for legislation and military contracts that favor the privileged and make the rich richer. President Bush is reported to be saying, rather proudly, that he will amass an election war chest of $200 million, with more to come. And the ruling political party in Congress continues to resist any change in the campaign finance laws that "give us the best government that money can buy!"

Franklin Roosevelt was hardly a saint, but his grasp of government seems now diametrically opposed to the vision of our incumbent federal leadership. In Roosevelt's second inaugural in 1937 he said:

> We have always known that heedless self-interest was bad morals; we now know that it is also bad economics.... The test of our progress is not whether we add more to the abundance of those who have much; it is whether we provide for those who have too little.

Nearly seventy years later, the figures of relative pay scales in our feverish wealth-accumulation system extend the disequilibrium between the rich and poor even further. Since 1980 the average chief executive pay has skyrocketed by 442 percent, to $1,364,524 annually. Average worker pay has inched up 1.6 percent, to $30,244 annually — which accounts for the fact that increasing hordes of the working poor cannot enjoy minimum benefits in a lavishly affluent culture at the top. Another comparison is equally shocking. For decades the figures on minimum wage and worker productivity rose in parallel. Between 1947 and 1973 worker productivity rose 108 percent, while the minimum wage rose 101 percent. No longer is there any just parallel. Between 1973 and 2000 worker productivity rose 52 percent, while the average wage *fell* 17 percent.[3]

THE WRITER RAM DASS tells of a recent trip to Hollywood, where he was hosted in the lavish upscale section of Brentwood. While being driven down a tidy avenue, he noticed that it was so quiet that he grew restive. There were no human beings in sight. Little plots of manicured grass grew between the sidewalk and the curb, but beyond the walkway were only high walls and electrically operated gates. On each narrow plot of grass a sign was posted by security providers that warned Armed Response. People who had made it to the top of wealth and external power felt the need to secure themselves behind bolted gates and armed guards. Power lives in fear of the powerless, while the powerless exercise their power to isolate and terrorize the powerful.

THE TRAGEDY OF THE MOUNTING DISTANCE between privilege and poverty is further exacerbated by a culture of violence that feeds on armed conquest as a patriotic virtue and gun-dominated TV and film entertainment. These realities are vivid emblems of an apocalyptic view of history. *Apocalypse* means "disclosure" or "revelation" — a great disclosure that concentrates on a sudden fiery and convulsive end of the world. The planet has only so many more heartbeats to live. Ironically, this is essentially a fundamentalist heartlessness. It is the bitter "good news" of fundamentalist conviction. It powers an exclusivist missionary activity and raises a perfervid expectation that "Jesus will come soon," spreading fire on earth. It also accounts for fundamentalism's heavy preoccupation with heaven and how to get there.

The principal proclamation is "Believe in the Lord Jesus and be saved!" Or "Belong to the church and be rescued!" It is God's design either to save *soon* only those who are committed to Christ as personal savior or to save *eventually* only the church of Jesus Christ and those who are evangelized into its fold. This represents the sharp exclusivist character of fundamentalist preaching and teaching — some of it impatient for an immediate world's end, some of it grimly patient for a victorious evangelism that will eventuate in a world-embracing Christian church. And it tends to be immune to the antiwar and social justice demands of the Old Testament prophets and the strong social thrust of Jesus's explosive condemnation of moral elitism, his nonviolence, and his embrace of justice for the poor and marginalized. Apocalyptic fundamentalism

also tends to scorn science as a dependable foundation for understanding God's will and work, retaining a
late-nineteenth-century rejection of science as seriously
deviate from Scripture. Science and religion, in fundamentalist theology, occupy frequently contradictory
categories of truth. Science is useful to fundamentalism in providing religion with the broadcast marvels of
radio, film, and TV, as well as sound amplifiers and air-
conditioning. But for an "end of the world" mentality,
science is an enemy of biblical truth about the brief time
allotment for world history and the need for immediate
repentance and amendment of life. Science and secu-
larism are often linked as enemies of the apocalyptic
view of history. This is emphatic in the case of fundamentalism's outrage with medical science's collusion in
abortion practices.

Fundamentalism is not without redeeming qualities.
The seriousness with which fundamentalism makes God
a living reality in individual and family life is greatly
to its credit. But, to their discredit most fundamentalist leaders ignore the prophetic social dimensions of the
biblical record and the ministry of Jesus, whose emblem
before the world is a Cross of total commitment to nonviolence as the way of humanity's deliverance from the
long scourge of war. Thus *fundamentalism can never serve
the world's longing for peace.* Moreover, it can never help
move the world from a pervasive adolescent addiction
to violence as the alternative to the emerging maturity
of the human project, a maturity that slowly supplants
the long-prevailing "male dominance" paradigm that
has brought the planet to the brink of death either by
nuclear holocaust or environmental rape—or both.

THE FAITH ALTERNATIVE to fundamentalism is an evolutionist understanding of God's will and action in the world. An evolutionist needs to be distinguished from a devotee of evolutionism. Evolution is a science-derived mechanism of creation entirely congruent with the "belief system" that rises from the biblical record where "the less is derived from the more." For the evolutionist, the initiative and design of evolution rises from the power of God: "In the beginning when God created the heavens and the earth..." (Genesis 1:1). "Then God said, 'Let us make humankind in our image...'" (Genesis 1:26), honoring the demonstrably transcendent and mystical dimension of human experience. By contrast, evolutionism is itself a "belief system." It ignores or displaces the biblical record and dismisses a divine initiative in the process of creation. In evolutionism "the more derives from the less." Over unimaginable time humanity rises from atomic dust, rocks, slime, frogs, and hairy mammalian forebears. Evolutionism, while claiming scientific foundations, seems less than good science for its lack of species-connective evidence. In its severest forms evolutionism regards the mystical (transcendent) dimension of human experience with some amusement, defining mysticism as beginning in "mist" and ending in "schism." However, both evolution and evolutionism are sharply distinguishable from creationism. The latter is also a "belief system" that disallows the extensive time-line of creation disclosed by archeology and paleontology, insisting on the scientific authenticity of the biblical time-line of six days computed by the learned Archbishop James Ussher of Ireland in the seventeenth century to have occurred in 4004 BCE. By its insistence on the brevity of the time-line of literalist biblical tradition, creationism is also less than good science. Therefore this deduction seems clear: science and religion can be friends in the evolutionist view of the world, but must be alienated in the views of both evolutionism and creationism.

Increasingly in our time science and faith have become mutually reinforcing by virtue of the quantum insights of modern physics. The new physics understands the universe as a living web of "interbeing," as the Buddhist monk Thich Nhat Hahn puts it. Nothing in God's pulsing cosmos is inert. The Jesuit paleontologist and mystic Pierre Teilhard de Chardin is a principal and poetic voice in bringing science and faith into partnership. In 1916, at the age of thirty-five he wrote:

> The world is still being created and in the world it is Christ who is reaching his fulfillment. When I heard and understood this saying, I looked around and I saw, as though in an ecstasy, that through all nature I was immersed in God."[4]

This is the pan-entheism of the long, mystic tradition of Christianity. It understands and experiences the presence and power of God in all creation. Science and spirit have become mutually reinforcing across many religious boundaries. Before his death in 1955 Albert Einstein wrote,

> A human being is part of the whole, of what we call the universe, a part limited in time and space. We experience ourselves, our thoughts and feelings, as something separate from the rest. This is a kind

of optical illusion of consciousness. This illusion is
a kind of prison for us, restricting us to our personal desires and affection for those closest to us.
Our task must be to free ourselves from this prison
by widening our circle of compassion for all living
creatures and the whole of nature in its beauty.[5]

Long before globalism emerged as a reality it became
apparent to Teilhard that a sea change in human experience was coming. In the 1930s he wrote essays on
what he called the "Planetization of Humankind"—the
rebounding and infolding of humanity on itself. For
Teilhard, and for growing numbers of believers across
the compressing world, evolution is creating a new and
uniting level of consciousness that, though furiously
resisted by a dominant militarist and fundamentalist
mentality, will irreversibly foster a "oneness" for which
the world is built in the purposes of God — and for
which the human spirit longs in its nearly universal
hope of peace.

The "irreversibility" of Teilhard's idealism is highly
arguable, even deniable, in light of the conquest and
retaliatory capability of nations with nuclear arsenals
and ambitions. But Teilhard was no airy optimist. He
faced squarely the power of evil, though he offended
Christian orthodoxy in defining it. As a theologian/
scientist, he held that there is but one evil. He named it
disunion. Teilhard meant the very thing that contemporary quantum theory affirms, namely that the cosmos
is essentially a single, unified, and pulsing interconnectedness, in which all entities need relationship and
intimacy for their fulfillment—from atoms to people to

the wheeling stars. What this worldview says is that evil is powered by the fears and pretensions that feed the arrogance of not needing one another across all divisions — and not caring for the interconnected fabric of life in the wind and the willows of the perishable earth. Evil for the evolutionist is that sinister force of fear that prohibits the grace of love and forgiveness that rebinds and reunites the sundered fabric of the web of life. Further, for the evolutionist, the great remedial power in the cosmos is the gracious admonition at the heart of God, who spins the stars and calms all the storms with this assurance: "Take heart, it is I; do not be afraid."[6]

CONCENTRATED WEALTH AND WEAPONRY do not cancel fear, nor do they succeed in securing us; *they only repress fear with lavishly expensive symbols of insecurity.* Fear is an inner reality that no elaboration of external securities can cancel. An internal dread can only be conquered by an internal power. God's sovereignty in the long view of history has the power to defeat despair and, it seems to me, is the deepest source of hope. The human spirit can be lifted and energized by the evolutionary calendar of the long trudge of humanity up and out of the twilight of human presence on our singular planet. Long-term history stirs hope for the world. A short-term apocalyptic otherworldliness cannot. By its very preoccupation with heaven, apocalypticism dismisses the world as expendable, arrogantly squandering its long project of life—about 4.5 billion years long.

The modern digs of archaeology and carbon-14 dating give rise to the estimate that at the nearest end of that long life line, or about 100,000 years ago, advancing human consciousness began to overspread the earth. Somewhere along the immense time-line of mammalian evolution the consciousness of primitive humanity erupted into self-reflection. This was the supreme moment of humanity's self-transcendence, and we became the beings *that know and know that we know.* My guess is that the eruption was probably communitarian, since evolution appears to proceed by populations rather than by individuals in isolation. Maybe some prophetic genius, joined by a community of excited interactive minds, began to see over the horizon of animal instinct that inherits a world and into the vast imaginative sky of human creativity that builds a world.

The timing of that early massive shift, or hinge of history, is impossible to pinpoint. The span of years is too great and our fossil evidence too scanty to suggest a time-definite point of transformation from instinct to reasoning. However, a great hinge of history since then is fairly easy to locate. It lies in the spread of years between the discovery of agriculture and the emergence of conquest empires like Egypt, Sumer, and Babylon. That shift in the human story occurred somewhere between 8000 and 5000 BCE. Hosts of us now believe that our own time in the long human odyssey is shaping into another immense and beckoning hinge of history. If this reckoning be granted, it is possible to mark three major turning points in the last 100,000 years. One hundred thousand years is very recent in terms of paleontology's estimate that hominoid forms began to appear as far back as four million years ago. Using only the hominid (distinctly human) evolutionary calendar, the first of the great turning points occurred roughly 100,000 years ago when self-reflexive consciousness erupted, the second about 10,000 years ago, and the third now.

I have assigned names to the eras between turning points that parallel the eras of modern humanity's individual development. This is arbitrary, yet descriptive and hopeful. The long era between the first and second turning points, 93,000 years by rough reckoning, I want to call the *childhood of humanity*. The much briefer era between the second and third turning points I want to call the *adolescence of humanity*, the era of expansion, invention and war that overlaps the era now aching to be born. This third era, the portentous era of our own lives, probably began hundreds of years ago but did not erupt into blinding nuclear visibility until August 1945. I call it the *maturity of humanity*. To name it so is to lean heavily on hope. It is to trust the capacity of "cunning humanity" to grow up. From years of reading in archaeology and paleontology, I believe it is important to think of these three eras in terms of power. The power to manipulate the inherited world has advanced by exponential leaps, until now the choice to use manipulated violence threatens the very existence of the planet as our only known resource base for life. Thus we could define our moment on the present swinging hinge of history as the crisis of violence. The crisis is substantiated by the fact that the twentieth century, just concluded, was the most violent one hundred years in all the accumulated centuries *put together* of human habitation since the appearance of our sapiential forebears.

As *homo sapiens,* we have been here about 100,000 years. This is a rough approximation of the span of years that "advanced" human species have been present on the earth. Neanderthals, with bigger brain cases than ours, preceded us Cro-Magnon types, but both types appear to have evolved in tandem, with many thousands of years of overlap. The evidence is scant, fragmentary, and even vigorously denied by apocalyptic religionists, but it mounts each year as the sciences of archaeology and paleontology continue digging and deducing. The *evidence of paleontology strongly suggests that for most of human habitation we have lived peaceably with one another.* In light of the best and most recent research, 93 percent of our 100,000 years as sapiential humans we have lived interpersonally in relative nonviolence. All but about 7 percent of the distinctly human years have been marked by the resolution of conflict in ways that preserve the peace. From what records we have of prehistory this news is momentous. It means that human types appear to have practiced relative intrahuman peace for nearly ten times as long as we have practiced war.

Actually, in the line of hominoid presence on the planet, a line extending about four million years, according to the most recent digs and paleontological research, a remarkably hopeful picture emerges. Harvard social anthropologist William Ury writes:

> If all four million years of human evolution were to be telescoped into a single twenty-four-hour day, the period of peaceable management and resolution of inevitable conflict would last through the

night, the morning, the afternoon, the evening, all the way, in fact, until just before midnight. The period we call history, filled with violence and domination, wars and empires, would last barely one minute.[7]

This deduction is made possible by the work of many scholars and researchers since World War II, especially that of Ury. His book, *Getting to Peace,* is a detective saga as he reports his personal on-site archaeological research in Africa. His deductions from his own and others' research make the claim that for most of the long years of human presence, we have known how to defuse and control the impulses of possessive animosities that lead to violence, largely by what he calls "third-party intervention." This means that, *while human conflict is inevitable, violence is optional*—if only we can learn again what our primal forebears knew and practiced in the early twilight of our earth time.

THIS IS THE LOFTY CHALLENGE to all leadership in our tightly interwoven world. It is a challenge to renounce the fear and fury of a scientifically insupportable religious apocalypse. It is a daunting challenge to live in the holistic bonding of science and faith. In the view of many quantum-oriented scientists, this is the beckoning light in an otherwise dark tomorrow. In his book *Life's Solutions,* Simon Conway Morris, professor of paleobiology at the University of Cambridge, writes,

Given that evolution has produced sentient species with a sense of purpose, it is reasonable to take the claims of theology seriously. In recent years

there has been a resurgence of interest in the connections that might serve to re-unify the scientific
worldview with the religious instinct. Much of the
discussion is tentative, and the difficulties remain
daunting, but it is more than worth the effort. *In
my view it will be in our lifetime.*[8]

Apocalypse is a creed of hopelessness for the human
project. By contrast, evolution is the science-derived and
biblically kindred stance of hope for a new world now
aborning. Although apocalyptic religion relies heavily
on the book of Revelation for its certainty of imminent
doom, that same document can be read with high hope-
fulness. Revelation is as much a forecast of new life for
the world as it is a message that God will soon abandon the human pilgrimage to the violent folly of fear
and rage. The dawning of a new human consciousness
is prophesied explicitly in Revelation, where it is written,
"See, I am making all things new."[9] When it is objected
by the wistful of our time that the world "is not the
same old place," the hopeful heart understands this as
a salute, not a lament. The "old place" can be what it
was in the childhood of human time—and yet new beyond imagining by the emerging forces of maturity on
the far side of our fear-driven violent adolescence.

This is not to suggest utopia, a Greek term that means
"no place." It is to hope for a conciliatopia. This is my
word for a world in which the practice of reconciliation advances upon the evil of disunion and fulfills the
inextinguishable longing of all life for justice, reunion,
ecstasy, and love.

So hope for a great sea change
On the far side of revenge.
Believe that a farther shore
Is reachable from here.
Believe in miracles
And cures and healing wells.

—Seamus Heaney

Chapter Five

Global Warming of the Second Kind

As unhappy as I am that war is upon us, I'm taking great comfort in what's going on in our world today. ...Now there are two superpowers: the United States and the emerging voice of the people of the world. All around the world people are waging peace. It is nothing short of a miracle, and it is working.

— Dr. Robert Muller, assistant secretary-general
of the United Nations, 1970–1985

THIS PERSONAL AND PUBLIC ODYSSEY is written many months ahead of the election of 2004, and no prediction as to the outcome of that event is ventured. It could go either way, depending on several factors. A heavy turnout of voters, especially among the economically deprived, would favor a shift in party dominance. Or if the occupation of Iraq were to continue to sour and job losses continue apace, the 2004 election could dismiss the present administration and bring in new presidential and congressional leadership. On the other hand, if the economy sustains a rebound, employment improves, and the Iraqi aftermath is pacified, the incumbent party would likely win reelection. Or if, God forbid, another massive terrorist assault would success-fully level some national icons, like the Capitol building or the Lincoln and Washington memorials in the au-tumn of 2004, the incumbent leadership would easily be returned to office.

Much is up in the air, but of one thing we can be cer-tain: the massive hinge of history is slowly swinging. It is swinging under pressure from two major sources. First is the rising momentum of nonviolence as a posi-tive problem solver. Second is the increasing pressure to halt and eventually reverse the tide of environmental degradation. Whether the great hinge will swing soon enough and far enough to sustain the imperiled human and planetary odysseys no one knows. But we can know both the peril and the promise. At the moment, given the immensity of nuclear capability in our own and other arsenals and our determined support for undiminished oil consumption by the incumbent administration, the peril looms far larger than the promise. This means that those who recognize the peril and who push hope-fully on the doors of tomorrow need one another as pilgrims of the promise. The spiritual exercises in the ap-pendix of this book are designed to cultivate hope and companionship in commitment to a finer future.

MEANWHILE, THE LITERATURE AND PRACTICE of active nonviolence and an enlightened discipleship to envi-ronmental protection both grow apace. This is what I refer to as global warming of the second kind.

Consider first the warming trend of nonviolence. To the charge that nonviolence is idealistic, the answer is, *of course!* Ideals are what energize the human spirit.

If nonviolence were not an ideal, we could not use it. Ideals are embodied in all the structures of freedom that Americans cherish. The erosion of ideals is precisely what sickens the American spirit and polarizes the electorate. The first victim of all violence, private and public, is the commanding ideal of truth. All regimes that exalt violence use deliberate lies as perverse instruments of power. Nazi Germany was awash in lies about Aryan racial purity and an adulterating Jewish conspiracy. The exposure of deliberate deceit by the administration as preparation for citizen support of the Iraqi war is an alarming sign of social and political decadence. Ideals are the driving energy of all social constructs of freedom, in both personal and public life: "You will know the truth, and the truth will make you free."[1] To his teaching on truth, Jesus added the cost of it by enduring vicious resistance to truth and by dying for its sake in nonviolent endurance, forgiving of his executioners. The Cross is a vile emblem of the most ruthless cruelty, which, by an embrace of active nonviolence, has since become the luminous symbol of the enduring power of God's all-inclusive love and mercy.

IT IS NO ACCIDENT that modern history's most forceful user of nonviolence as an instrument of political change called his method *satyagraha*. Mohandas Gandhi translated the word as "truth force." Sometimes he interpreted the Hindi term as "soul force" or "love force." The word is actually Gandhi's own invention, combining two Hindi nouns, *satya* and *āgraha*. Gandhi as a religious leader used truth force in the political arena, saying that those who oppose the entrance of religion into politics do not know the meaning of religion. Martin Luther King Jr., following Gandhi, used religious conviction as a force for working nonviolently in the American political arena. King's doctoral studies at Boston University rose from the life and work of Gandhi. In the successful nonviolent social change wrought by Dr. King and his followers, Gandhi's life and witness were the forces that lay behind the American civil rights achievement. In one of King's most memorable addresses he gives vivid voice to the power of nonviolence.:

> [To] our most bitter enemies we say, "We shall match your capacity to inflict suffering with our capacity to endure suffering. We shall meet your physical force with soul force. Do to us what you will, and we shall continue to love you. We cannot in good conscience obey your unjust laws, because non-cooperation with evil is as much a moral obligation as is cooperation with the good.... One day we shall win freedom, but not only for ourselves. We shall so appeal to your heart and conscience that we shall win you in the process, and our victory will be a double [triumph]."[2]

Gandhi's influence spreads now across the world, making truth force the energy for political reform in such recent nonviolent victories as in formerly Communist Russia, formerly apartheid South Africa, and formerly violence-torn Ireland. Gandhi attributed his learning about nonviolence to the Christian scriptures that he read while a law student in England as a young man. Returning to India, with an important interlude in South Africa, he knew intimately the dominant white political and military forces that ruled the so-called Christian nations of his experience. Some of his biographies contend that he considered converting from his native Hinduism to Christianity. Those that I have read[3] are clear that he decided to remain a Hindu because of the dissonance between the teachings of Jesus and the value systems of the "Christian" nations that he knew well. He is reported to have said, "Everybody knows that Christianity is a religion of nonviolence except the Christians." This is akin to a conviction of Abraham Lincoln, who was never baptized a Christian, though he worshipped at the New York Avenue Presbyterian Church in Washington, D.C., and quoted the Bible in his inaugurals and official statements. When asked why he refused to be baptized, Lincoln regularly replied that he would gladly accept the sacrament and join the church that practiced the clear commandments of Christ that we love God and one another. Still, despite the broad failure of Christian populations to live by the truth force of satyagraha, nonviolence blossoms and grows as a political engine of reform and renewal. The sanctity of the ballot, under suspected attack in the 2000 election by a regime of conquest by violence, is precisely an instrument of satyagraha, of truth force. *The ballot belongs to the people, not to the government, and its protection as an instrument of citizen possession is of critical importance to American freedom and the defeat of imperialist aggrandizement.*

ENVIRONMENTAL REFORM also blossoms across the world, especially in the northern hemisphere, where the crisis of global warming is most exacerbated by petroleum usage. Environmental reform will continue to grow, I believe, no matter what the outcome of the next election. Only a nuclear catastrophe could halt its gathering momentum.

Since April 2001 my wife and I have had a new set of wheels in our garage, a Prius. It is a small emblem of global warming of the second kind — like the first green shoots of daffodils that brighten the face of February. Born in Japan under the auspices of the Toyota Motor Company, Prius combines the motive power of electricity and fossil fuel. It is an engineering breakthrough of such ingenuity that the suitcase-size engine in front intermittently recharges the oversized battery in the ample trunk behind the rear seat. The trunk will easily hold two large pieces of luggage (or two huge golf bags plus umbrellas and shoes). Not only does the battery get an occasional boost from the engine, but also the friction-induced heat from the brakes generates a recharge. Result: no need for external recharging and up to 55 miles per gallon, with exhaust emissions of only 10 percent of its larger garage mate. The Prius is also a jackrabbit, rocketing on command and cruising easily at 65 on an interstate.

There is something pleasingly "spiritual" about that car. It stands as an outward and visible sign of an inward and spiritual grace — an irreversible shift in the soul of contemporary humanity. It is the shift from careless consumption and pollution of the planet to a caring appreciation of our living and vulnerable resource base. The Prius is only the first mass-produced "hybrid" vehicle to honor the cries of the earth. Much more is to come. Honda Motors also markets a practical hybrid car, and

General Motors and Toyota have stepped beyond blind competition to collaborate in the design and production of fuel cell vehicles that reduce carbon emissions to zero.

All this represents a spiritual reformation — a transaction in our advancing human consciousness — and it comes at what looks like the last few minutes of opportunity to preserve life "unto the seventh generation." *Consciousness* is the emerging word that makes it possible to speak of the inner life without confusing the conversation with religious talk. Multiplying numbers of us who rejoice in global warming of the second kind appreciate the word *spiritual* because we believe in a deep distinction between religion and spirituality. Spirituality is primary. It is rooted in human prehistory as a genetically coded impulse, whereas religion is the later developed organization and codification of our advancing spiritual development. Spirituality is etched into human prehistory as far back as Neanderthal burial practices of 100,000 to 60,000 years ago. Our early forebears added both implements and ornaments to the graves of their dead — clear signs of primordial belief in an afterlife. Archaeology has uncovered gravesites that include hunting and cooking tools, and even fossilized flowers as emblems of caring remembrance.

NOT ONLY DOES THE SCIENCE of the "ancient" (paleoanthropology) testify to deep spirituality, so also does the science of the very new (quantum physics). Both sciences add the weight of their empirical evidence to the reality of inborn and advancing spirituality. Quantum theory insists that everything is connected to everything else in a web of life. The newest scientific insights reverse the older discrete "parts and pieces" reduction of the universe in Newtonian mechanics, and the new perception of cosmic interdependence means that any action that diminishes others in the great web of life diminishes the diminisher. A person is lessened as an individual for any contempt of, or heedless violence inflicted upon, any other entity in the order of life.

In an interlocking system, what is done to others is done to one's self. This is the foundation of the Golden Rule that unites the ethics of all the religious systems in the human family. In Islam it reads, "None of you is a believer until he desires for his brother that which he desires for himself." In the Buddhist tradition it reads, "Hurt not others in ways that you yourself would find hurtful." Instantly this universal ethic mandates the emergence of political arrangements that honor all lives in the intricate scale of life. That we are far from perfection in achieving the ideal is no reason for despair. *It is not the goal that counts nearly so much as the advance we make in approaching it.* The question for our time is therefore not: Have we created a relationship-serious global civilization that cherishes all forms of life? The real question is: Are we serious about moving toward such an outcome in our common life in the earth? While the outcome is problematic and in the distance, the process is clearly under way, and the process is what counts in a Creation still being created.

THERE IS AN AXIOM from the Hindu tradition to encourage hope. Called kami yoga, it means that the key to success in any endeavor is to avoid preoccupation with the outcome in favor of attention to the process. This translates into the wisdom of good golf that urges, "Keep your eye on the ball!" The key word in the title of this chapter is a "process" participle: *warming.* Not *warmed,* as if the process were completed; *Warming* carries the same process force as our familiar word for a house or a public structure. We call these things buildings, never builts, even though they may be completed in the sense that the builders have left the property. But the fact is that they are never finished. Every building is described in process terms, never in the language of finished products. So too is the earth, the planet of God's entrustment to human hearts and ingenuity. All life is one huge process, *and it is never over.*

The current political leadership in America is bent on policies that shield consumerist market capitalism against challenge by the rising tide of environmental passion. The same leadership presses for gargantuan sums for military investment, to the impoverishment of American children and their education in deteriorating schools manned by underpaid teachers. *But this is a predictable part of the process.* Pressure to change any destructive addiction, personally or publicly, will always arouse denial and resistance. Talk to any member of Alcoholics Anonymous or AlAnon — or to any of us in the privileged sector of American society who struggle against the addictive blandishments of our rich materialist life style.

Meanwhile, the beat for liberation from cultural captivity goes on, and it mounts. In all sectors of American enterprise there are leaders who pull the bell ropes that ring out for radical change, from the practice of power as dominance to a conviction that real power lies in partnership, negotiation, reconciliation, and love—love of the natural order and love of one another across all boundaries. Dr. Margaret Wheatley, a good friend and author of best-seller business books, writes:

> What gives power its charge, positive or negative, is the quality of relationships. Those who relate through coercion, or from disregard of the other person, create negative energy. Those who are open to others and who see others in their full-ness create positive energy. Love in organizations, then, is the most potent source of power we have available.[4]

This leads directly to the current shift from power structures of hierarchy to circular network models of interaction in organizations, in which leadership is exercised as a power center of participation in responsibility and decision making.

KNOWING THAT SPIRITUALITY is stamped indelibly into our genetic coding, and that to be human is to be spiritual, I wonder how the different religions of the world can add their ancient and honorable power to the "fusionist" energy of global warming of a second kind. The great religions are the most enduring of all the world's institutions. The oldest among them emerged in the mists of many centuries before Jesus. Hinduism, Buddhism, and Judaism are all pre-Christian. Most of the remainder are centuries older than constitutional democracy, and nearly everybody knows that Abraham and Moses were famous long before Jesus of Nazareth.

The renowned biblical scholar Marcus Borg sometimes refers to Christianity as "a way of being Jewish" — which is precisely accurate historically, since the Christian movement grew directly from Jewish roots and half or more of the distinctly Christian scriptures are of Jewish authorship. This is a liberal way of getting at the problem of religious tolerance and cooperation. But religious tolerance in a globalizing culture is already fiercely resisted by the male-dominant fundamentalist sectors of several world religions, which is simply *another natural and inevitable expression of resistance to the irreversible unifying process.*

Christians of biblical seriousness can be troubled by a verse in John 14:6, which many interpret as forbidding any relativising of Christian exclusivity: "No one cometh unto the Father except by me." Dr. Borg writes that the key to freeing the text from rigid exclusivism lies in the introductory language of the passage. "I am the way...." says Jesus in anticipation of what follows. A way clearly implies a path, a journey, a process, not a verbal formula or a dogmatic prescription. In other passages Jesus vividly sets forth his way — the way of death and rebirth (resurrection). In an earlier encounter with the text in John's Gospel, Jesus is remembered as instructing a highly placed Jewish seeker, one Nicodemus, a preeminent member of the prevailing Jewish hierarchy who initiated a question about gaining eternal life. Jesus answered unequivocally, "You must all be born again."[5] Rebirth implies dying to an old and familiar way and being given a new and finer way of life — a life in allegiance to the indiscriminate love of God as mirrored in the life of Jesus, whose mercy takes him to the Cross.

Marcus Borg recalls a story he heard about a sermon preached by a Hindu scholar in a Christian seminary several decades ago. The text on that occasion included the "one way" passage in John 14:6. "This verse is absolutely true," said the scholar. "Jesus is the only way. And that way, of dying to an old way of being and being born into a new way of being, is known to all the religions of the world."[6] The way of Jesus is a universal reality of life, known to millions who may have never heard his name. Thus the "way" of Jesus as the "truth and the life" is not a set of beliefs about Jesus, but a path of transition and transformation—from an old "rule and regulation" preoccupation in an exclusivist way of being and behaving to a reborn life of compassion, justice, healing, peace, and self-giving. Behold the beauty of this understanding: *it offers common ground to fundamentalist and fusionist Christians alike.*

When Billy Graham urges "giving your life to Christ," he is not prescribing anything uniquely Christian, only using Christian language to declare a universal truth. It is the truth that a longed-for rescue from a life of self-destruction in any one of a hundred addictions to "fear" and "me first" comes of dying to an old self-preoccupied and fearful way of life and being "born again" to a new way of fulfillment.

WHEN THE UNIVERSALITY of this truth is seen, not just personally but prophetically in terms of social reform and rebirth, it will warm the fires of a new world now in process of aborning. What it means in global terms is clear: that the way to a new world of economic justice and environmental sustainability is the way of the Cross. It means the process of dying to an old way of *untruth* — the unsustainable way of inequitable consumption of the planet's diminishing resources. It means rising to a new way of being a human family in the intricately interwoven web of life. It means dying to a greed-driven competition while accepting honorable competition as useful in adding zest to life. Even more, it means living into the dream of God and the dream of all healthy human aspiration for a finer world of justice, compassion, and peace. It means dying to dread of change and rising to embrace the overriding challenge of this swinging hinge of history: that we live into the advancing process of

1. simplifying our lifestyles;

2. reinventing our industrial systems and our fuel and power sources;

3. eliminating the monetary grip of special interests on our political processes;

4. disavowing war as a costly, counterproductive, historically outmoded, and violence-compounding conflict-resolution mechanism; and

5. resolving that human presence on this exquisite planet shall cause no callous and ill-considered harm to persons or to our living partners lower on the scale of consciousness.

The fact that substantial and increasing numbers of the human family are committed to the above is why it is possible to talk about global warming of the second kind. Of course, such a new vision of life raises fierce friction, but friction always raises the levels of energy. We need not worry that current reality is loaded with manifest improbability. Visions are never justified by their plausibility. The human spirit goes for great dreams not because they are plausible, but because they are irresistible.

Chapter Six

The Future of Power

Today we all stand at a turning point when changes in how we view our world and how we live in it are more important now than they have ever been before.

—Riane Eisler, *The Power of Partnership*

THE STRUGGLE FOR OUR FUTURE is not between the forces of capitalism and communism. Both represent powerful male-dominant forms of social and political organization, whether in America or China or some other dominator society. The real struggle is between a world society oriented primarily to competitive domination and one oriented to collaborative partnership. In other words, the future of the human project will be decided by the choice between a force-based ideal of human governance and a sharing-based ideal of human and environmental interaction. The crisis of choice could not be more pressing. The human project will remain in peril as long as the world's singular superpower conceives of its leadership as arming itself with nuclear instruments of global domination. As long as power is understood as dominance, or the capacity to compel compliance, any lethal weaponry anywhere is a constant source of disequilibrium and threat to the peace and survival of the world. This has been so since the beginning of the long history of "power over" as being of far greater advantage than "power with." But the advent and stockpiling of nuclear weaponry mark the terminus of that advantage, both to its possessor and to the rest of the world.

Henceforward, if the planet's long history of life-giving abundance is to continue, power must be re-conceived at its roots. The power paradigm of dominance must yield to the sustaining superiority of a power paradigm of partnership, or the end is near. The issue is just that simple, and the ominous tragedy is that the most powerful nation in the world has not yet learned its truth and cannot summon the will to act accordingly. Still, there are nations that do see and act on the truth, and their number is climbing. Costa Rica, for example, which dismantled its entire military establishment in 1948, has been joined by several nations that have either abandoned their military or installed strict weapons and gun control. They include Brazil, Canada, and Japan, where only the police are legally armed, except for hunters and self-defense forces.

SO THERE IS HOPE. Hope lies in a fierce paradox: *the very stridency of the domination policies of the world's singular superpower may signal its radical insecurity, its own threatened sense of displacement.* The American presidential election outcome of 2000 can be seen as symptomatic of desperation in the right-wing electoral constituency in which power is understood as subjugation and control. The bid of the Bush candidacy for the office of president actually failed in the popular voting. Only by the perceived manipulation of the balloting in Florida and closely divided partisan decision making in the Supreme Court do the Bush forces now lead America into lavish indebtedness, scorn of social and environmental priorities, and a contrived war in which the victims of conquest, so far, refuse to be conquered. The hopeful ingredient in this picture of force-based dominator excess is that it appears to be arousing its own repudiation in the political arena, where aggressive opposition preparations are under way long ahead of the next election—a political phenomenon new in our time. But the conservative desperation in 2000 can be counted on to escalate in 2004. Although nonviolent and collaborative feminist values are on the rise across the world and male dominance is diminishing as a value system, the dominator grip on the levers of control in America is formidable and determined. A more liberal election outcome in 2004 may not be enough to shift the balance of power. There may be no way short of revolution to dislodge the fierce force of apocalyptic right-wing ideology.

Still, the saving revolution seems to be incubating. If so, its power will be primarily spiritual — a rising recognition that violence-based power can never again secure the future. By contrast with contemporary violence, it was nonviolence that propelled the future for thousands of years in the prehistory of humanity, succeeded roughly 8,000 to 10,000 years ago by a rising tide of violence that has secured only temporary and unstable eras of peace in recorded history down to August 1945. Since then American military violence has not won a war, even though we have deployed troops and advanced weaponry in Korea, Vietnam, the Persian Gulf, and now Iraq—and find that we must keep them in most of these tinderbox locations at astronomical cost with no strategies for exit. *Violence as a problem solver is totally bankrupt,* although it thrives in the folly of societies addicted to its thrall.

FOR THE SAKE of an ongoing human presence, the addiction to violence must give way to nonviolent approaches to modern conflict, as seen in India under Gandhi and in America under Martin Luther King Jr. Such resounding victories of nonviolence open the door to a possible future that restores to human use the wisdom of our ancient and nameless forebears deep in prehistory. That wisdom is the basis for hope.

The final curtain may still come down on the long and troubled pageant of life on earth. But *hope is the future tense of faith and love*. These are the triumphant values of the human spirit, and they will endure under God, no matter what carnage we commit upon our home in the heavens. So I invite a look at what we know about the innate human capacity for nonviolence.

The Childhood of Humanity

Somewhere in the years of my enthrallment with archaeology and paleontology it slowly dawned on me that, as a species, humanity has been recapitulating the life process of each individual. In a favorable life development each of us moves through three basic phases: (1) an extensive symbiotic oneness with family in childhood, (2) a prolonged and normally rebellious struggle into a competitive "twoness" in adolescence, that sooner or later, if we are lucky, mellows into (3) a phase of collaborative wholeness that wears the wondrous face of maturity. The mystic power of phase three is the compassionate impulse that looks out upon any "other" as a beautiful, flawed, and forgiven mirror image of one's own unfinished self. This is the foundation of the universal ethic enshrined in all the world's religions: that "we do unto others what we would have them do unto us." This is also foundational to the newest quantum science and to the most ancient edicts of faith, because humanity is fashioned into such interconnected wholeness that what we do to others we are bound to do to ourselves.

GROWING NUMBERS OF SOCIAL HISTORIANS confirm my hopeful conviction that the human odyssey lives now at a critical juncture. We are at a point in time that resembles the eighth to sixth millennia BCE, when humanity stretched up and out of a relatively peaceable childhood into a rising crescendo of adolescent bravado. Now, at the apex of human violence that marks the hinge between the twentieth and twenty-first centuries CE, our species has entered upon the immense struggle to forsake our teenage swagger and armed carnage in favor of a human maturity never before seen in any grand planetary measure. This beckoning maturity is the music that summons us from over the horizon ahead — a song that we have only begun to sing that cherishes the earth as our mother and one another as sisters and brothers across all the boundaries of living species, races, creeds, sexual differences, and national fealties. This is the hope that fires my life in its now steady diminishment into old age. Each morning I pray to God that I may be a tiny force in advancing the promise of a new and peaceable planet for my children and their children and their companions at every level of life in a world that comprehends and cherishes its oneness.

Three researchers and writers have instructed me in the ways of our forebears who lived without warfare. In the order of my coming upon them, they are Richard Leakey in his book *Origins,* Riane Eisler in *The Chalice and the Blade,* and William Ury in *Getting to Peace.*[1] Of the three, Eisler's book has had the most resounding impact on contemporary readership. *The Chalice and the Blade* had been through twenty-five printings and been translated into more than a dozen languages when I bought my paperback copy in 1996, a volume now almost falling apart from revisits to its pages.

In a variety of ways all three researchers contend, or imply, the priority of feminine values and attributes during the long stretch of peaceable years to about 8000 BCE. Eisler is especially firm in this assertion. Societal forms took the shape of matriarchy for generations. Lineage was traced through the mother, not the father. When male-female "partnering" eventuated in marriage, the husband left his family to make his home with his wife's people and took his wife's family name. For countless generations human society was matrilineal and matriarchal. The basis of matriarchy lay deep in the natural perception that human life rises from the female womb. The fertile earth itself was easily perceived as the Great Mother who provided fresh water, succulent tubers, vegetation, and animals for the hunt.

This is an instinct so deep in human consciousness that modern language retains the primitive designation for the planet as Mother Earth. As spiritual sensitivity developed and icons were fashioned as worship emblems, all the symbols of divinity were uniformly feminine. Excavated clay and pottery figurines portray exclusively goddesses, with emphasis on the unique physicality of female organs: greatly enlarged breasts and exposed vaginal orifices.

THE RISE OF THE FEMINIST MOVEMENT in our time is clearly a sign of hope that a peaceable world is within the circle of possibility, although apocalyptic right-wing spokespersons are frequently contemptuous of contemporary feminist gains, such as the Reverend Jerry Falwell with his instant assignment of blame for the 9/11 terrorist assault on feminists, environmentalists, and other liberal forces. Still, the liberating forces are alive and well, as seen in the racial equality movement and the growing environmental drive. The feminist movement, in my view, undergirds and empowers them all. What this means in deep historical terms is that contemporary achievements of feminine freedoms in political and business leadership represent recovery, not innovation. Feminist values have been in the ascendancy before, and they stimulated the momentum of social evolution and preserved the peace of the primitive world. While their resurgence in our time means a recovery, not a new invention, some important innovations are in order. The innovations called for are adjustments in the "traditional" patterns of child care, homemaking, and family economics. The recovery of feminine values also impacts the workplace with the emergence of collaborative patterns of leadership as contrasted with dominance and traditionally competitive relationships. Difficult as these interpersonal adjustments may be, they represent the reascendancy of feminine forces and instincts that forecast a recovered capacity for peace in the human project. This would be a recovery that, if it can come in time and with adequate persuasive power, promises to preserve the world against incinerating warfare and sustain our human presence against extinction.

The importance of William Ury's more recent research is that it makes a lie of the once widely held assumption that humanity is genetically programmed to violence. Ury spent months doing on-site examinations of caves in South Africa, places from which earlier deductions were made about violent intrahuman behavior on the evidence of crushed and precisely pierced skulls. His digs and deductions prove that most, if not all, fragmentations of human fossil evidence are the result of either collapsing cave formations that crushed human burial locations or the rapacity of animal prey that turned lethal claws and jaws on the hunter. In substantiation of these deductions there have been found no implements of intrahuman warfare that could be carbon dated before 7000 to 5000 BCE. This is true for all locations of the most recent archaeological digs in South Africa, Europe, and the Middle East.

Riane Eisler reports on the extensive work of James Mellaart, a British archaeologist whose excavations concentrated on the plains of Anatolia in eastern Turkey.

Mellaart unearthed two Neolithic urban sites dating from the seventh millennium BCE, Catal Huyuk (c. 6500–5000) and Hacilar (c. 5700–5000). Three features of discovery are especially important. First is the fact that, although these societies were goddess-based in religious orientation and matrilineal in family formation, they were not repressive of the male half of humanity. From all the evidence of art, religious symbolism, and social organization, the childhood of our humanity understood power not in terms of domination, but in terms of responsibility — responsibility for the whole of society. Human relationships took the form of linking modes of shared responsibility in contrast to our later ranking modes of power and privilege. Second, to substantiate the early and prevailing linking modes, the houses in these dense urban clusters were all much the same size and shape. Nowhere were there sharp distinctions in the household life of the community — no mansions, no palaces — nor was there evidence of wretched underclass housing. Prehistoric habitation was shaped to commonality and shared responsibility for the advancing human project. Third, the artwork and frescoes of Catal Huyuk and Hacilar never idealized weapons and warfare, in stark contrast to the friezes and statuary of male-dominant Egyptian culture that succeeded the Neolithic era.

This is the incontestable evidence of an early human social and political arrangement of collaborative partnership. This is also the scientifically incontestable argument that demolishes the prevalent dire assumptions that humanity is genetically programmed to violence. We are *not* so programmed! Deeper in our human makeup than competitive aggression are all the everyday expressions of love and peaceable interaction that make marriage and child rearing the norms of life in the face of all the competitive stresses that work against our longing for peace. Deeper in our human makeup than the violence of nations is the compassion that opens our hearts to suffering across all boundaries, including the boundaries between species that are lovingly breached in compassionate rescue of abandoned and abused animals. These are the deeper etchings of genetic tracery in our God-given souls, and they persist as both hope and challenge. The primordial social and political constructs that emerged from these profound blueprints of the heart can still be coaxed into operative norms — if there is time to grow beyond the era of our once natural and now demonically obsolete adolescence.

The Adolescence of Humanity

So, the urgent question: What happened to change a peaceable, feminist social order to one that abandoned linking modes of human interaction in favor of ranking and ruthless modes of both individual and communal behavior?

Speculation abounds. We do not know precisely. Richard Leakey contends that the discovery and exploitation of agriculture started the decline. He calls the cultivation of land the "original sin," in the sense that it developed into a grasping materialism that gradually destroyed the social paradigm of mutuality and rages now as ruthless male-dominant competition for power

and advantage. This deduction has many marks of authenticity, but it is moderated, perhaps even corrected,
by evidence that 6,000 years later than the discovery
of agriculture certain advanced matriarchal and nonviolent societies on the mainland of Europe and on the
island of Crete were grounded in vigorous agricultural
economies. Leakey appears to hold too limited a view.

Riane Eisler holds a different conviction from Leakey.
Her supposition is that the peaceable cultures of Old Europe and the Middle East were gradually overrun by
warrior tribes of horsemen from regions farther east,
the Kurgan people from those parts we now call the
Asian steppes and Mongolia. These invaders apparently
were nomadic bands roaming the less desirable fringe
areas of the globe, seeking vegetation and water for
their herds. "We have nothing to go by but speculation
on how these nomadic bands grew in numbers and in
ferocity over what span of time," writes Eisler.[2] However, at a point in time about 5000 BCE, researchers
begin to find evidence of what James Mellaart calls
"a pattern of disruption" in the Old European cultures of cooperative and orderly social structures. The
ferocious male-dominant invaders came in waves according to another archaeologist and social historian,
Marija Gimbutas, on whose research Eisler relies. The
first Kurgan wave can be traced to 4300–4200 BCE,
the second to 3400–3200 BCE, and the third to 3000–
2800 BCE. The Kurgans were an Indo-European stock
of heavily male-dominant and warlike social habits, the
type idealized in modern times by F. W. Nietzsche and
Adolf Hitler as the only pure European race. Ruled by

powerful priests and warriors, they imported into previously peaceable societies the male gods of war and the mountains.

There were other fierce invaders of the same period. Most noteworthy were the nomadic Hebrews, who came from the desert areas of the south. The early strata of the Hebrew Bible reflect the violence-prone male dominance of the nomadic Semites, whose rulers were castes of warrior priests and whose edicts often called for slaughter and pillage. Passages in Joshua draw a hideous picture of male-dominant carnage: "...Joshua and the men of Israel had finished inflicting a very great slaughter on them....Afterward Joshua struck them [the conquered five kings] down and put them to death, and he hung them on five trees. And they hung on the trees until evening."[3]

What the Kurgan and Hebrew-Semitic invaders had in common was a dominator model of social organization. Their systems featured male superiority, male violence, and generally a hierarchic and authoritarian structure of governance. "Power with" was gradually and ultimately overturned by the "power over" paradigm of relationships. Competition replaced collaboration as the norm of governance and the spur to personal achievement. Later Sumerian and Babylonian military regimes reflect the ascendancy of competitive "twoness" as compared to the familial oneness in the childhood of human evolution. Regimes of violent conquest and oppression are heavily symbolic of the dominant values of our own epoch — a prolonged period of adolescent behavior and social patterns.

Heavy economic advantage accrues to the powerful in a male-dominant "power over" culture, with corresponding increases in poverty and sharp disequilibrium in the advantages of the rich over the poor. These are clearly descriptions of current circumstance as incumbent political leadership in the United States makes its male-dominant power the controlling paradigm of economic distribution and budget priorities. Although we claim a democratic political, social, and economic identity, America bears an updated and ominous resemblance to ancient Sumer, Babylon, and the invading Hebrew tribes that offer a presumed "divinely biblical" blueprint for a predatory modern Israeli takeover of Palestinian lands.

STILL, ADOLESCENCE BRINGS redeeming qualities, both in personal and in long historical terms. It is a time of flowering creativity. Our adolescent era, while extensive in the sense that it occupies all of recorded history, is relatively brief as compared with the immense stretch of time that marked the childhood of our species. In spite of its brief duration, our adolescence represents a veritable explosion of innovation and discovery. Total contempt and rejection of these last 10,000 years are therefore out of order—as indeed most of us have some of our own shameful adolescent excesses to embrace in forgiveness. When we consider, for example, the glory of ancient Greece, its exalted thinkers, its political innovators, and its commanding architecture, our frustration with species adolescence is mitigated by an abounding appreciation. Those ugly/beautiful years, like our own personal breakaway years from oneness to twoness, have been seasons of human blossoming. When you know that the Colossus of Rhodes once stood astride the Hellespont, or when you have felt staggered by the magnificence of the cathedral of Chartres, or when you read the perilous construction history of the Brooklyn Bridge or behold the giant images of visionary American leadership graven in the granite of Mount Rushmore—when these bold stretches of human daring and imagination bedazzle you, then history becomes a sturdy foundation for hope. Adolescent "twoness" is like all great truth: it wears the face of paradox in its blend of savage violence and soaring creativity.

The paradox bespeaks the commanding challenge of our time: *our dazzling conquest of nature may be our very undoing.* Two achievements signal the possibility of human extinction. The first of these exploded in the atomic incineration of nearly 300,000 Japanese in 1945, mostly women, old men, and children. Cunning, aggressive, and violent humanity has a weapon that makes its use in warfare an Armageddon. The second achievement emerged with the forecast of a silent spring by Rachel Carson in 1962, when environmental disaster loomed on the horizon. Again the paradox: our conquest of nature may be the very force that conquers the conquerors. Still, history is the ground of hope.

The saving move from violent twoness to mature wholeness began long ago, at a point in our pilgrimage when it became apparent to prophetic souls that a competitive, materialist grab at life would ultimately secure neither fulfillment nor life itself. The Buddha awakened to this truth around 600 BCE. At about the same time Hebrew prophets added moral force to the plea for a noble and peaceable humanity. Later still it came to commanding flower in a Mediterranean Jew whom half or more of the world honors as Jesus of Nazareth: "Blessed are the meek; they shall inherit the earth.... How blessed are the peacemakers; they shall be called the children of God...."[4] And further still: "Love your enemies and do good to them who hate you...."[5] The way from species adolescence to holistic maturity has beckoned humanity by keen voices of velvet and steel for generations, perhaps long enough to grow now into the highest human consciousness that has ever peopled and secured the planet. Such a growth would constitute an evolutionary leap of epic proportions. Although current American political leadership wears a warrior face, signs are near at hand that the human project is poised on the nonviolent horizon of its high fulfillment in an era of maturity unseen except in the prayers and pains of a long-incipient set of saints.

The Maturity of Humanity

The wholeness of a transcendent heart in the human species has begun to beat. Its primary attribute is penitence. Guarantors of a human and planetary future are intuitively repentant. The repentance called for by the world's greatest Peacemaker involves remorse, surely, but true repentance does not begin with remorse. Nor does it end there, unless remorse results only in mood swings instead of new behavior. Changed behavior, concrete action, is always the test of true repentance. It begins, I believe, in seeing the truth and telling the truth. The best remembered myth that Jesus invented as a carrier of his teaching recapitulates precisely the threefold saga of human evolution compressed in this chapter. The childhood oneness of the Prodigal Son is presupposed in the achievement of his adolescent two-ness, when he asks for his inheritance, with which he swaggers out to indulge the fancies of an expanded life horizon. Finding lavish indulgence a mirage and the road to inner emptiness, the adolescent moves through a life-giving turning about. In the pain of self-alienation he confronts the truth as he comes home to his created selfhood. As Jesus told the tale in Luke 15: "...he came to himself and said, I have sinned...."[6] He *saw* the truth and returned home to *tell* the truth and rose from an encounter with forgiveness a whole man.

In this capital myth from the genius of the world's singular peacemaker we have the enduring ingredients of the spiritual revolution that can move the human pilgrimage through the ominous uncertainty of this second great hinge of history and onto a farther shore beyond the vain violence of our species adolescence. While violence is vain, hope is never so. Pockets of mature truth telling are emerging all across a maturing human world. They practice a Lenten-like truth telling and remorse over our adolescent violence against women, against the nonwhites of the human family, against animals, against the innocent earth, against nations like Vietnam, against the children of Iraq by economic sanctions and military carnage, against the starving children of the planet's southern hemisphere. Again, the wholeness of a transcendent human heart has begun to beat across the world. Let it beat in a rising tempo at home and in the churches and synagogues of

America. Especially the churches. Let the churches in-
stall prayers and Lenten exercises that go far beyond
the private penitence of Ash Wednesday litanies. Let the
churches fashion penitential disciplines reflective of the
monstrous social sins against one another in the human
family and against our having suffocated the gift of life
on earth. Let the churches be quick to understand and
confess the pervasive sins against our created solidarity
with one another, or these bastions of spiritual privacy
will face the slow demise of institutional irrelevancy.

THE SONG FOR OUR MOMENT in history is one that
lingers in our hymnals and our hearts: "O God our help
in ages past, our hope for years to come...." Hope is
aroused by the new nonviolence sprung from spiritual
resources that sees in any other person, especially in an
enemy, the flawed and lovable mirror image of one's
own unfinished and forgiven self. This is to practice the
peaceable ethic enjoined by the One who gave us the
story of the Prodigal come to himself: "Love your enemies, do good to those that hate you...."[7] This remains
almost antithetical to raw personal impulse and to conventional public behavior, but experience proves it to
be self-preserving and world saving. It is the high ethic
encouraged by the new nonviolence that mounts like a
rising tide in our time.

THE ACCELERATING RECORD of human history makes it
increasingly clear that nonviolence is the saving alternative to the brutal and obsolete cost of armed warfare.
Most recently, in April 2003, we witnessed a rising
crescendo of popular street demonstrations around the

world in protest of the American-led preemptive war against Iraq. Now, in 2004, there rises an outpouring of organized resistance to the costs and carnage of American political and military strut.

ALWAYS THERE WILL BE PROBLEMS in the parade of life, and they multiply now with too many leaders and far too many people holding two outmoded and devastating worldviews. First is the worldview of late-nineteenth-century fundamentalism that rises from an apocalyptic twist on an old religion and assumes that the history of God's business with the world began with an act of creation in 6000 BCE and glories in anticipation of the world's early demise for the sake of a privileged elect who will be raptured on high to eternal bliss. The second is the worldview of an older mechanical science that glories in reducing the cosmos to parts and pieces, seeing them in disconnection in order to rearrange them for manipulation—and for ultimate rearrangement in a nuclear nightmare that will send the saved to heaven. *New fundamentalist religion and old Newtonian science thus work together to perpetuate our species adolescence — and our demise in nuclear incineration.*

But our problems in the parade of life are now newly amenable to positive comprehension and solution by leaders and people who hold two very different and more hopeful worldviews. They are, first, a vitalizing recognition that God's work in the cosmos stretches through countless ages, perhaps as long as multiple billions of years, and that life in its myriad expressions on the planet is our sacred responsibility to cherish and preserve as part of the work of justice and love. Justice and love: these two virtues at the foundation of goodness go together, because justice is simply love writ as large as life. Second is an emerging displacement of old Newtonian mechanics in favor of a new comprehension of creation as an interwoven web of pulsing heartbeats, from the tiniest atomic subquark to the most distant galaxy of wheeling stars, with the human soul as the living receptor of this vast God-given holograph of interwoven beauty and activity. In contrast to the fundamentalist and hopeless collaboration of new religion and old science, there has emerged in our prophetic time an antithetical and saving combination of new science and old religion. Quantum physics and prophetic spirituality now work for the preservation and fulfillment of God's vision of the oneness of life.

The French Jesuit Pierre Teilhard de Chardin was enthralled with union as the power to overcome evil and simultaneously to act as the mysterious source of enhanced individuality. He explained this paradox of unity in diversity with his axiom "Union differentiates." What he meant was that, in both the physicality and spirituality of evolving life, the greater the fusion of individual components to make an advanced species, the greater the enhancement of distinctive individuality in that species. This accounts for the distinction we see clearly in the higher animals. No two of our dogs and cats and horses are precise duplicates. When it comes to humans, as highest on the scale, each of us is decidedly unrepeatable. Even more, we know that as great love is given us, in the bonding of mother and child and the bonding of women and men married well and long, our distinctive individuality is not only prized but made safe for distinctive expression.

Later than Teilhard came the American Jewish physicist David Bohm, who perceived the cosmos as a good and godly oneness. He, like Teilhard, held fast to the paradox of individuality in the holographic unity of life and said of all entities in creation that "there is separation without separateness."[8] If you lock your fingers to make a tight bowl in front of you, a small picture of Bohm's holograph is fashioned. The fingers are clearly distinguishable, but you have created an interwoven oneness of your two hands that will hold water until you tire. May God write upon all our hearts the holistic truth of the high human maturity now preparing to flower into fullness: that *we are one people in one planet with one future.*

Hope and the
Sword of the Spirit

God help us to change;
To change ourselves
*   and to change our world;*
To know the need of it;
To deal with the pain of it;
To feel the joy of it;
To undertake the journey
*   without understanding the destination;*
The art of gentle revolution.

—Michael Leunig

TWO CONTEMPORARY WRITERS are keen clarifiers of the way ahead for the human odyssey. From a blend of spiritual sensitivity and historical scholarship, they encourage hope that America is furnished with a quality of spirit that can turn the nation from its pursuit of peril to a change of course that could lead the world in the promise of peace. They are David Loye in *Darwin's Lost Theory of Love* and Jonathan Schell in *The Unconquerable World*.

Loye has done a scrupulous computer search of Darwin's second great book, *The Descent of Man* which followed by twelve years his first and more influential volume, *On the Origin of Species,* written in 1859. In Darwin's *Descent of Man,* Loye found almost no references to the governing assumption of Darwin's first book, namely the "survival of the fittest." This is the doctrine on which is based the conviction that aggression and violence are genetically programmed into essential human behavior. Darwin's second book concentrates on human evolution in contrast to the total drama of evolving life that he reported in his better known first volume. In the explicitly human *Descent of Man,* Loye found only two references to survival of the fittest, which makes competitive aggression the engine of evolution. In bright contrast, he noted ninety-five references to behaviors Darwin described as "affiliative," "sympathetic," "collaborative," "affectionate," and "loving." This stands as an important Darwinian corrective to the long-held popular understanding of human behavior as irremediably violent to the core. Evolution, for Darwin, moves irreversibly in the direction of an ever-higher morality, which is already incipiently universal, as shown in the convergence of religious morality in simultaneous versions of the Golden Rule in all the major religions of the world.

The central point for the findings and vision of Darwin's second half (*Descent of Man*) is how, out of evolution, there has been given to us the capacity to drive the whole of this special planetary venture toward what moral sensitivity urges upon us. Evolution in our species arrives at what the greatest among us can become, but which all of

us bear within ourselves in potential—the capacity
for being the scouts or venturers in new directions,
or *the evolutionary outriders for our species.*[1]

Thus the latest Darwinian studies underscore and confirm the more recent discoveries and deductions about
humanity's tomorrow from research in archaeology
and paleontology.

Jonathan Schell has researched the citizen protests of
organized warfare since Vietnam, the first Gulf War and
the worldwide demonstrations against the armed invasion of Iraq by the second Bush administration. He has
named this rising tide of popular protest the "People's
War" as a counterforce to unilateral nation-based warfare. Schell illustrates the power of this counterforce by
reporting a high-level conversation in 1968 about the
continuing failure of our military meddling in Vietnam.
The incoming U.S. president is talking to his choice for
secretary of state: "When Richard Nixon was preparing to take office as president, he asked [Dean] Rusk,
'Where was the war lost?' Rusk answered, 'In the editorial rooms of this country.'"[2]

Schell uses opposing political forces to illustrate the
realism of a hopeful future. He points out that in the
contest between descending dictates from the top and
the ascending power of citizens from below it is the
aroused power of citizens that proves the case for what
Abraham Lincoln forecast as imperishable from the
earth: government of the people, by the people, and for
the people.

The nonviolent activity of the people is not the
same power that flows downward from the state by

virtue of its command of the instruments of force, and yet the two kinds of power contend in the same world for the upper hand, and the seemingly weaker one can, it turns out, defeat the seemingly stronger.... For it is a frequent mistake of the powers that be to imagine that they can accomplish or prevent by force what a Gandhi or a Martin Luther King can inspire by example. The prosperous and mighty of our day still live at a dizzy height above the wretched of the earth, yet the latter have made their will felt in ways that have changed the world, and will change it more.[3]

My hope is fired for having seen my own Episcopal Church grow young while I have grown old. The reverse process to my aging began in the late 1950s with our divisive embrace of Martin Luther King Jr. and his crusade for civil rights, and it climaxed in 2003 by the equally divisive decision of both houses of our General Convention to ratify the election of an openly gay man to be bishop of New Hampshire. In this half century of my ministry we have become more like the early church in the brave embrace of St. Paul's dictum that "there is no longer Jew or Greek, there is no longer slave or free, there is no longer male or female: for all of you are one in Christ Jesus."[4] Now we have added "There is no longer gay or straight."

Paul's dictum rises not simply from the intuitive leap of a spiritual and intellectual giant. It is solidly grounded in his transforming conversion from Jewish rule-oriented rage to his ardent embrace of the embryonic Christian community, as well as in his allegiance to the historic decision of the church's first assembly to act inclusively. In the fifteenth chapter of the book of Acts, the revolutionary new Jewish movement was faced with the decision as to whether the growing company of uncircumcised Gentiles, who had joined their ranks, needed the Jewish mark of circumcision in order to be fully included. The assembly said emphatically that no such exclusionary ritual of membership would be required. Gentiles needed to observe some dietary niceties of Jewish tradition, but their identity as Christians depended not on an outward sectarian ritual. Rather, it depended on the inner bonds of a new allegiance to Jesus the Christ — and the moral courage to demonstrate the force of that allegiance in new behavior in a hostile world.

BEFORE 313 CE, the Christian community was entirely pacifist in the heavily military and occasionally persecutory Roman Empire. A Christian in the Roman army would have been a contradiction in terms. After 313, when the Emperor Constantine co-opted the Christian movement as a politically solidifying strategy, the infant church grew steadily more approving of the violence of warfare. Cultural captivity began to overtake the Christian community. The abandonment of pacifism was completed a century later by the towering work of a once-profligate genius who had been converted and was baptized in the Christian faith. St. Augustine, noted earlier in this book for his dubious doctrine of original sin, turned his great intellect to the moral question of war and invented a debatable doctrine. From his scholarly knowledge of Plato and the Greek philosophers, along with his fear of barbarous warriors who threatened the invasion of his North African diocese, he fashioned a moral defense of warfare that has since become known as the just war theory. It has been used and misused since to justify the Crusades, the Inquisitions, and the "war to end all wars." Most recently it has been misused to sanction a preemptive strike against a ruthless head of state in Iraq suspected of arming his nation with a few of the same weapons that our nation keeps at the ready by the thousands in silos and submarines for first-strike use. The present administration precisely reflects the Jungian doctrine of projection in concentrating on all evil elsewhere while absolving our nation of any responsibility for stressed and shattered relationships.

SINCE THE KOREAN WAR America has developed, albeit unevenly, an imperial resemblance to Rome in its ambition for aggressive dominance. By sharp contrast, in the same half century the Episcopal Church has moved more and more in the opposite direction. Clearly we have stepped up our use of the inclusionist power of Servanthood that marked our life in the blossoming years nearest in time to the One for whom we are named as Christians, nearest in time to his teaching that "all who take the sword will perish by the sword"[5] nearest in time to his admonition to "love your enemies and pray for those who persecute you."[6]

Often these days we hear arguments that seek to justify American militarism by quoting Jesus in scriptural isolation from all of the above and in particular neglect Christ's acceptance of his execution by the prevailing cultural forces of church and state. Some contemporary justifiers of war turn to the single verse in Matthew that reports Jesus as saying, "Do not think that I have come to bring peace to the earth; I have not come to bring peace, but a sword."[7] Always it has been easy to mishandle the Bible by quoting, out of context, passages that seem to support an action or a point of view that violates the larger meaning of Scripture. Seen in the totality of Jesus's ministry and teaching, *this verse is a precise description of the real sword he wielded.* The sword he drew was a moral weapon against the very values of exclusivity and injustice that brutalized the poor and fused an unholy alliance of ritual religion and Roman imperialism to nail him to a bloody gibbet. In this critical time of being fed a patriotic religiosity by a Washington conspiracy, we need to be crystal clear. That single verse of Scripture is a thundering indictment of the conventional value system that drives our present American war making. The context of that verse is a bull's-eye description of the divisive consequences of a nonviolent value system in conflict with any prevailing system that supports the status quo. "I have come to set a man against his father . . . and one's foes will be members of one's own household."[8] Nothing could be more up-to-date than this sweeping text from Matthew.

MY FATHER AND I were at sharp odds over the civil rights movement in the 1960s. He was a dedicated racist, contemptuous of black people as inferior specimens of humanity. I had been released from any such imprisoning prejudices by participation in the movement led by Martin Luther King Jr. My father and I were locked in the very controversy Jesus promised when he spoke of the wrenching conflict of exclusive and inclusive value systems. Quite as he promised, Jesus "set a man against his father." On other value issues than race this was also true. My father was a lifelong Episcopalian, and he and I could not speak of the radical changes in his cherished old prayer book without arousing verbal conflict. Among the larger circle of my relatives, I have an elderly kinswoman who regards as politically treasonous my abandonment of a proper Republican upbringing. As for my church family, there are hosts of faithful laity and clergy of the Episcopal Church who might gladly have me consigned to oblivion for writing this book. Jesus's demands for social justice and his peacemaking priorities do indeed wield a sword!

Still, by the grace of God it remains possible in strained relationships to honor one another in efforts to understand the reasons for differing convictions as being held in honesty — and from sharply differing personal histories. Providentially there exists no commandment of God that we must be "correct." There is only the reconciling mandate that we love. The enduring commandment is that we love God, self, and one another in compassion and forgiveness. Love is the fulfillment, not only of the law, but also of the deepest longing in the human heart to be loved for one's distinctive self.

My father and I, though never at peace over certain political issues or ecclesial policies, were never at a great distance from one another in a love that blossomed more and more as he approached his death at age eighty-three. I am certain that, could we talk now, our mutual capacity to grow in love would bring us together in great patience with one another, perhaps even to the point of seeing the wonder and strength of our Episcopal Church to have used its primordial power in Christ to be more and more inclusive. Servanthood, not dominance, has been the developing posture of the Episcopal Church in all the fifty-four years of my ordained ministry. We have responded in nonviolence to the just demands of black sisters and brothers, women in Holy Orders, liturgical reform, and same-sex oriented men and women as disciples and leaders among us. Our next step into the moral courage of the first three centuries of the Christian odyssey will be our nascent readiness to repudiate war. War can no longer stand as a solution to any public human conflict. It remains for churches of the Christian enterprise to recover the war-resisting grace and grit of our vibrant youth and to declare ourselves, by creed and deed, churches of peace.

THIS SMALL BOOK begins with a dedication to the world-transforming spirituality and courage of Mohandas Gandhi. It closes with a statement of realism from his profound enlightenment:

> We may never be strong enough to be entirely non-violent in thought, word and deed. But we must keep nonviolence as our goal and make strong progress towards it. The attainment of freedom, whether for a person, a nation or a world, must be in exact proportion to the attainment of non-violence for each.[9]

Appendix

Resources for Participation in Global Warming of the Second Kind

Thaw with her gentle persuasion is more powerful than Thor with his hammer. The one melts, the other breaks in pieces. —Henry David Thoreau

Preamble

I UNDERSTAND THIS TIME IN HISTORY to be a turning point in the human odyssey that magnifies both peril and promise. The heightening of human power has raised both the danger of planetary catastrophe and the possibility of a global family at peace with one another and the living environment. Rejoicing in the interconnectedness of all life, I face the peril by choosing the promise—working to counter the forces of fear, violence, and predatory nationalism that threaten to foreclose the global future.

In allegiance to the challenge in all religions that "we do unto others what we would have them do unto us," I commit myself to a spiritual discipline in service to relationships, using the resolutions, spiritual discipline,

135

litany, and prayers that follow. (Note: The resolutions are adapted from the work of Rodney Ross Romney, a retired Episcopal priest of Idaho Falls, Idaho, and printed with his permission. The spiritual discipline and what follows are the author's.)

The Resolutions

1. *I resolve to live as a citizen of the world.* God has already blessed America, calling on this nation to share its security, its goodness, and its abundance with people everywhere. The United States is not God's chosen, any more than any other social/political entity. It is the world that God loves.

2. *I resolve to resist all legal systems that deliberately destroy life, such as capital punishment and war.* The United States, among the major industrialized nations, is the only one that continues to kill its citizens as punishment for their crimes. As a nation, we once took worthy pride in the knowledge that we never committed a preemptive strike against another nation. We need to recover that posture of true strength, or to restore the old name of our military establishment as the Department of War.

3. *I resolve never to be a part of a religious institution that excludes others or that views itself as the sole approach to truth or to God.* The human spiritual impulse precedes by many millennia the appearance of specific religions. In their distinctive richness the religions should be understood as later organizations and

codifications of a spiritual instinct that appears very early in the evolution of consciousness.

4. *I resolve to live as openly as possible to the presence of God in the life of the world.* As a Christian, I embrace the truth of Christ, as declared to Nicodemus in John 3:3, who invites an offering and surrender of my life for daily rebirth in the Spirit.

5. *I resolve to give of my resources to those movements and institutions that seek to embody such resolutions as these.* I recognize that, created as we are in God's image, we are built to give and that life's deepest satisfactions lie in habits of generosity.

6. *I resolve to live as a peacemaker in the world, and to offer discernment, understanding, and reconciliation wherever conflict calls forth the need for peacemaking.* This resolve applies as much to political adversaries as to enemies of human solidarity. I cannot be an instrument of peace and live in determined animosity with anyone. Such generosity of heart I recognize must come from the grace of God, not from any personal power—except the resolve to rely for daily rebirth in the Holy Spirit.

A Twelve-Step Spiritual Discipline

1. I am given life and love by Power not my own.

2. I am also wounded by life and often hindered by a failure of courage.

3. I seek healing and release from fear.

4. I see in Jesus of Nazareth, and in the prophets of many faith traditions, a Servanthood to humanity's welfare and the peace of the world.

5. In the temptations, death, and resurrection of Jesus, I see the conquest of fear and the victory of nonviolent power used for serving.

6. In the risk of personal commitment, I offer my life to Jesus Christ and accept God's call to Servanthood as my vocation.

7. In truth about myself, I acknowledge my waywardness from love and my misuse of power in deceptions and personal ill will.

8. I ask God to deliver me from all corruptions of power, trusting to be delivered from fear and given the courage to live truthfully.

9. I give thanks for the grace of forgiveness that frees me to love myself and all others in the interwoven web of life.

10. I practice prayer as a waiting upon that Grace, believing that in success and failure God wills our good and enlarges our capacity for Serving.

11. As a leader, I hold a vision of power used for justice, nonviolence, and peacemaking, striving to shape accordingly the systems of human interaction that I can influence—at home, in the workplace, and in the social/political order worldwide.

12. As a servant, I choose to love God by loving life in the world and by practicing integrity for myself, compassion toward others, and care for the earth as home for all that lives.

A Litany for Envisioning a New World

Refashion our minds, O God, to a new way of thinking, that seeing the peril in our power to halt the human odyssey, we commit to the promise of life for all that lives.

In your compassion, Lord, hear our prayer.

Reconcile our hearts to one another across all boundaries, that human diversity may be experienced as enrichment, and differences honored as leading to wiser action.

In your compassion, Lord, hear our prayer.

Sensitize the governments of the world to the folly of violent conquest that has led all of history's adventures in empire to ultimate decadence and demise, teaching all who aspire to leadership of the nations the enduring wisdom of collaboration and Servanthood.

In your compassion, Lord, hear our prayer.

Hasten the momentum of nonviolence that has emerged in our time, that human ingenuity may be turned to the preservation of the earth and our economies reordered to the urgent needs of the human family.

In your compassion, Lord, hear our prayer.

Kindle in each of us a resolve to dismantle our private arsenals of violence: our greed and thanklessness, our rage and grievances, our hatreds and all our shifting of blame.

In your compassion, Lord, hear our prayer.

Enliven the faith communities of the world with a rebirth of welcome for all sorts and conditions of humanity, moving us to reorder our lives and our loves to such simplicity and goodwill as preserve the earth and make for peace.

In the name of God, Creator, Reconciler, and Empowering Spirit. Amen.

A Prayer for the President of the United States

God our governor, by whose gift of freedom your people have evolved democracy as a political structure for our common life, instill in our president, George, a sense of servanthood in wielding the powers of leadership on our behalf. Confirm his conviction of divine call to his high office that he may seek your will in all things, and that the finest of our traditions may be preserved for sharing across the human family. Hold the president, and all of us, to the hope that a global embodiment of justice and peace is now aborning, and that when we listen with wider care we can hear that new world's eager heartbeat. Amen.

A Prayer for Servant Leaders

Eternal God, who tarries oft
    beyond the time we hope for,
    but never beyond the time appointed,
    from whom comes in due season
    the truth that cannot lie,
    the counsel that cannot fail,
Make us faithful to wait upon our watchtowers
    for what you would say to us.
Gird our hearts against all fear that our servanthood
    may gird the hearts of all
    whom you give us to lead.
In the name and power of your Servant Son,
    Jesus Christ our Lord. Amen.

Notes

Foreword: The Politics of Peril and Promise

1. William L. Ury, *Getting to Peace* (New York: Viking, 1999), 35.

2. Abraham J. Heschel, "History" in *The Prophets* (New York: Harper and Row, 1962), 1:159–86.

3. Matthew 5:43–44.

4. Riane Eisler, *The Power of Partnership* (Navato, Calif.: New World Library, 2002), 188.

5. Luke 6:41.

Chapter 1: Saints and Sinners

1. See below chap. 6, pp. 5–7.

2. J. Philip Newell, *Listening for the Heartbeat of God* (London: SPCK, 1997), 49.

3. *American Book of Common Prayer* (New York: Oxford University Press, 1928), 6.

4. *American Book of Common Prayer* (New York: Church Hymnal Corp., 1977), 79.

5. *Thayer's English-Greek Lexicon* (New York: Harper Brothers, 1886; rep. New York: American Book Co.), 660.

6. John Shelby Spong, *Here I Stand* (San Francisco: HarperCollins, 2000), 336.

Chapter 2: Competition Superseded

1. Mark 10:43–44.

2. William L. Ury, *Getting to Peace* (New York: Viking, 1999), 95.

3. *Turning Point* 4, no. 1, published by the Institute for Servant Leadership, Asheville, North Carolina.

4. Daniel Yankelovich and associates, *Work and Human Values* (Cambridge: Cambridge University Press, 1983), 6–67.

Chapter 3: Leadership as the Exercise of Power

1. Matthew 4:4.
2. Matthew 4:5, Revised English Bible.
3. H. Vanstone, Hymn no. 585, *Hymnal of the Episcopal Church* (New York: Church Hymnal Corporation, 1982).
4. Matthew 4:9.
5. Mark 8:35.
6. Luke 10:27–28.
7. Romans 13:8–10.
8. John 14:27.

Chapter 4: Apocalypse and Evolution

1. Riane Eisler, *The Chalice and the Blade* (San Francisco: Harper-Collins, 1997), 246.
2. *National Catholic Reporter*, May 23, 2003, 14.
3. Reported in the *Charlotte Observer*, June 23, 2003.
4. Pierre Teilhard de Chardin, *"La vie cosmique"* (1916), quoted in *The Teilhard de Chardin Album*, ed. Jeanne Mortier and L. M. Auboux (New York: Harper & Row, 1966), 37.
5. Albert Einstein, Heartland Institute, Edina, Minnesota, Vol. 3, May 2000. A personal letter answering a nineteen-year-old woman who was grieving the loss of her sister and wanted to know what the famous scientist might say for her comfort. Written March 4, 1950.
6. Mark 6:50.
7. William L. Ury, *Getting to Peace* (New York: Viking, 1999), 56.
8. Simon Conway Morris, *Life's Solutions* (Cambridge: Cambridge University Press, 2003), 328, emphasis mine.
9. Revelation 21:5.

Chapter 5: Global Warming of the Second Kind

1. John 8:32.
2. Martin Luther King Jr., *The Trumpet of Conscience* (New York: Hodder and Stoughton, 1968).
3. Judith M. Brown, *Gandhi: Prisoner of Hope* (New Haven: Yale University Press, 1989); William L. Shirer, *Gandhi: A Memoir* (New York: Simon and Schuster, 1979); M. K. Gandhi, *An Autobiography* (Boston: Beacon Press, 1957); Louis Fischer, *Gandhi: His Life and Message* (New York: New American Library, 1954).

4. Margaret J. Wheatley, *Leadership and the New Science* (San Francisco: Barrett-Kohler, 1992), 39.

5. John 3:7, Revised English Bible.

6. Marcus J. Borg, *Reading the Bible Again for the First Time* (San Francisco: HarperCollins, 2001), 216.

Chapter 6: The Future of Power

1. Richard E. Leakey and Roger Lewin, *Origins* (New York: Dutton, 1977); Riane Eisler, *The Chalice and the Blade* (San Francisco: Harper-Collins, 1997) (see notes to chap. 4 above); William L. Ury, *Getting to Peace* (New York: Viking, 1999) (see notes to foreword above).

2. Eisler, *The Chalice and the Blade*, 43.

3. Joshua 10:20–26.

4. Matthew 5:7, 9.

5. Matthew 5:44.

6. Luke 15:11–24.

7. Luke 6:27.

8. David Bohm, quoted in Joseph Jaworski, *Synchronicity* (San Francisco: Barrett-Kohler, 1996), 79.

Afterword

1. David Loye, *Darwin's Lost Theory of Love* (San Jose, Calif.: Excel, 2000), 202, italics mine.

2. Jonathan Schell, *The Unconquerable World* (New York: Metropolitan Books, 2003), 96.

3. Ibid., 231, emphasis mine.

4. Galatians 3:28.

5. Matthew 26:52.

6. Matthew 5:43–44.

7. Matthew 10:34.

8. Matthew 10:35–36.

9. *Peacemaking, Day by Day* (Erie, Pa.: Pax Christi, 2001), 6.